SETTING

BY

JACK M. BICKHAM

WRITER'S DIGEST BOOKS
CINCINNATI, OHIO

ABOUT THE AUTHOR

Jack M. Bickham taught professional writing at the University of Oklahoma for twenty-two years before retiring in 1991 to write full time. He is the author of more than seventy-five published novels, including *Twister*, *The Winemakers* and five novels published so far in a suspense series for Tor Books. He has written extensively for *Writer's Digest* magazine and his titles for Writer's Digest Books include *The 38 Most Common Fiction Writing Mistakes (and how to avoid them)* and *Scene and Structure*. He and his wife Louanna live in Norman, Oklahoma, where he is at work on three more novels.

Setting. Copyright © 1994 by Jack M. Bickham. Printed and bound in the United States of America. All rights reserved. No part of this book may be reproduced in any form or by any electronic or mechanical means including information storage and retrieval systems without permission in writing from the publisher, except by a reviewer, who may quote brief passages in a review. Published by Writer's Digest Books, an imprint of F&W Publications, Inc., 1507 Dana Avenue, Cincinnati, Ohio 45207. (800) 289-0963. First edition.

This hardcover edition of *Setting* features a "self-jacket" that eliminates the need for a separate dust jacket. It provides sturdy protection for your book while it saves paper, trees and energy.

Other fine Writer's Digest Books are available from your local bookstore or direct from the publisher.

99 98 97 96 95   7 6 5 4 3

Library of Congress Cataloging-in-Publication Data

Bickham, Jack M.
    Setting / by Jack M. Bickham.
        p.   cm.—(Elements of fiction writing)
    Includes index.
    ISBN 0-89879-635-0
    1. Fiction—Technique.   2. Setting (Literature) I. Title. II. Series.
PN3383.S42B53   1993
808.3—dc20   93-32510
                                                  CIP

Edited by Robin Gee

Nancy Berland's Setting Research Form is used with permission of Nancy Berland.

CONTENTS

1. Why setting is important • *1*
   How casual decisions may ruin a story
   How to develop the correct professional attitude
   toward development of your story setting

2. Presenting sense impressions • *8*
   Why sense impressions are vital
   How to deliver them to the reader

3. Presenting factual material • *19*
   Why facts are important
   How to deliver them to the reader

4. Fudging facts: When it's okay to stray from truth • *28*
   How to know when facts aren't necessary
   Knowing when it's okay to lie
   How to know when the truth is not enough

5. Setting in specialized stories • *38*
   It pays to know if your reader has set expectations

6. How setting acts as your story backbone • *48*
   Using setting to unify the story

7. How to use setting to advance plot • *62*
   Setting can make things happen and increase
   tension

8. How setting affects character • *71*
   Choosing the right setting-character match
   Using setting to enhance character credibility
   Using setting to change a character

9. How setting adds to story meaning and vitality • *85*
   Setting: A source of story ideas
   Setting and story meaning

10. Setting and viewpoint: It's how you look at it • *94*
    How viewpoint affects setting
    Finding the effective vantage point

11. Setting the mood: How setting viewpoint creates atmosphere • *101*
  How setting affects story atmosphere
  How setting contributes to your story's mood

12. Showing setting during movement and action • *110*
  How to show setting during movement and action
  How to describe setting without slowing the story

13. The story behind your setting • *125*
  How history and attitude link
  How both relate to setting—and everything else
  The importance of cultural/regional attitudes

14. Setting and style • *133*
  Using precise language in settings
  How to present strong, vivid settings
  How to get the words right

15. Exercises to sharpen your settings • *141*
  Practice, practice, practice

16. A program for further study and growth • *150*
  Keeping a setting journal
  Increasing your awareness
  Asking setting questions
  Developing your own resources

Appendix 1
Research resources and techniques • *155*

Appendix 2
Nancy Berland's setting research form • *165*

Index • *170*

CHAPTER 1

WHY SETTING IS IMPORTANT

SETTING IS A TOPIC seldom discussed at length in writers' workshops or addressed in any detail in texts for creators of fiction. Like the weather, it's mentioned in conversations, but considered entirely out of our control. Yet setting is a vital component of any story, and it does involve a body of technique which you can learn and use to improve your creative work.

Story setting is even defined too narrowly in those few texts which do consider it. It is not merely the physical backdrop of the tale. It may also include the historical background and cultural attitudes of a given place and time, the mood of a time, and how the story people talk. Also tied closely to setting may be such details as the author's style, a period's traditions, and the kind of story the writer wishes to relate.

All of these factors must dovetail properly with the story's plot, its characters, the theme and the desired general emotional tone of the piece if the finished fiction is to "work" for the reader.

Many classic tales are classics precisely because all these factors fit together perfectly. Most can scarcely be imagined in a different setting. Consider, for example, how profoundly different DeFoe's *Robinson Crusoe* would be if the author had chosen to have his hero shipwrecked on a barren arctic rock, rather than upon a tropical island. Could the story have been told at all in such a different setting? Would Dickens's *A Christmas Carol* have the same kind of impact if set in the English countryside? Or would the movie classic *High Noon* work emotionally for an

1

audience if it were set in an early-day English colony—or in a big city in the year 1993?

These are perhaps extreme examples, but you will discover, as you think about it, that setting does more than provide a framework within which the story is told. It makes some things possible, other things quite impossible. In a traditional Old West setting—to use another extreme example—one cannot have the hero leap onto a jetliner. By the same token, a detective in a gritty contemporary urban scene can hardly track his suspect the way Natty Bumppo might have done in one of the *Leatherstocking Tales*. Even character language can be a part of setting, or be tied to it. The kind of character talk that might be appropriate in an urban police mystery could destroy the credibility of a traditional historical romance because people in different places and times speak so diversely.

The moral: When you choose setting, you had better choose it wisely and well, because the very choice defines—and circumscribes—your story's possibilities.

In addition to its importance in terms of credibility, setting also contributes enormously to the general feeling or tone of a story. It creates a mixture of story mood, character feeling, and general ambience which eventually (in stories that work) become as much a part of the appeal and sense of "rightness" as the plot, characterization, or any other factor. Hemingway's *A Farewell to Arms* simply would not work if set in the Vietnam era, for example, because the emotions—so right in a novel of World War I—aren't at all appropriate for a story set a generation or two later. And of course the historical and cultural context of many recent suspense novels could only be believed if clearly dated in the period prior to the demise of the Soviet Union. If set "today," they simply wouldn't work because recent history has changed the feeling of the era.

The setting of a story can affect the author's wording—the writing style, too. Compare, for example, the opening of a novel like Daphne du Maurier's *Rebecca*, a gothic-baroque romance, with that of a contemporary thriller like *Darker Than Amber*, one of the Travis McGee novels by John D. MacDonald.

Rebecca begins:

> Last night I dreamt I went to Manderley again. It seemed to me I stood by the iron gate leading to the drive, and for a while I could not enter, for the way was barred to me. . . .

While the Travis McGee book opens this way:

> We were about to give up and call it a night when somebody dropped the girl off the bridge.

The romantic backdrop of *Rebecca* fits perfectly with the dreamy, cadenced quality of its prose—a style which would not fit at all in a John D. MacDonald novel. And the opposite, of course, is also true. In both cases, the setting dictated style as well as many other story factors.

Given the importance of a story's setting, it is surprising how often it is selected with little thought—just popping into the writer's head as part of the original idea, and never seriously examined thereafter. Even more amazing is how casually many writers treat setting in all its aspects.

This book is an attempt to change all that.

THE CONTRIBUTIONS OF SETTING

Writers generally recognize that good handling of a proper setting can "decorate" a story, thus enhancing its color and general appeal as well as making it more convincing. Less often realized, however, are the following additional contributions setting can make:

- intensification of reader involvement
- enhancement of story unity
- tightening of plot structure and/or intensification of suspense
- motivation or explanation of character
- clarification of theme
- excitement of the writer's own imagination

While we will look more deeply at most of these aspects, it may be well to consider each of them briefly at this early stage, to provide you with an overview of what is to follow.

Reader involvement may be intensified by proper handling of setting because physical, sensory descriptions of the story world allow the reader to experience those surroundings through his own imagination—as if he were "really there," seeing, hearing, breathing, tasting and feeling the world of the tale. Vivid, evocative physical description of setting can transport the reader into the story's universe. The reader may also derive an additional sense of involvement and satisfaction if he is given, as part of the setting, factual data which fascinates him and makes him feel he is learning something.

This kind of involvement and possible satisfaction not only predisposes the reader to be friendly to the writer, and generally relaxed, it also makes him more likely to believe the story's plot and characters because he is already having a pleasurable experience from the setting, and believes in the story world.

These are not minor advantages for the writer. She should always be alert for ways to soothe, please and enchant the reader, because a friendly reader is more apt to accept uncritically other aspects of the story.

Unity is another element upon which setting can have an obvious favorable impact. A story line may involve complex developments affecting a wide variety of characters; the issues may become very complex; there may even be multiple viewpoints and story lines taking place in different levels of the society. Yet a consistent setting can provide an unchanging backdrop against which even otherwise unrelated story developments or characters will be seen as related simply because they are taking place on the same stage.

Thus the physical setting can provide a unifying background scenery. The consistent tone of language and general story atmosphere which grow out of the physical setting also provide a sense of unity. For example, once an atmosphere of gothic horror has been established, even the innocent play of children in the "great, gloomy house" may become frightening for the already-enchanted reader, who would not otherwise see the children as in any way scary or threatened.

Plot or suspense can be advanced and complicated by setting. As one example, suppose your tale is about a wagon master who is leading a train of Conestogas across the prairie toward distant mountains. Your descriptions of the subtly changing scenery as the mountains become nearer act as a physical "scorecard" showing how the story is advancing toward its ultimate conclusion. If the reader knows that hostile Indians await in the mountain pass ahead, your repetitive mention of the mountains will become a drumbeat of suspense.

Similarly, the emotional atmosphere in an example cited earlier, the movie *High Noon*, was a vital component of the story's effectiveness. Some might quarrel with my definition of atmosphere as part of setting, and argue that the atmosphere *grew out of* the setting. I would reply that in a vivid setting, atmosphere can become so palpable that it seems to assume an identity of its own. Whichever side you might come down on concerning this distinction, I think you can readily see that atmosphere can hardly be considered without relating it to setting, however you choose to describe setting. In *High Noon*, the town's fear and the citizens' cowardly indifference served to isolate the hero more and more as time passed and the moment of crisis loomed; they became as real as the heat and the endless horizon. Without the atmosphere of fear, suspicion and cowardice, the repetitious plot — the hero repeatedly seeking help and being turned down — could have been meaningless and insipid.

Character is significantly linked to setting. The seafaring, whaling world of *Moby Dick*, for example, is crucial to an understanding of Captain Ahab and his mad quest for the white whale. Outside of the specialized setting Melville defines, Ahab's obsession makes no sense at all. And consider poor Amos Herzog in Saul Bellow's classic *Herzog*. The title character could hardly be believed outside the gritty, decaying, smog-plagued urban landscape in which he is depicted. He is a product of that environment, and his motives and thought processes are inextricably driven by it.

One of my own novels, *Twister*, concerns an outbreak of tornadoes across the eastern two-thirds of the United States similar to the actual outbreak of April 3, 1974, when dozens of storms wreaked hundreds of millions of dollars in damages and injured or killed scores of Americans. In this book, the setting of the storm system was the novel's very reason for being, and a cold front spawning many tornadoes actually became the central character in a good portion of the book. Setting seldom becomes this central in a novel, but the fact that it can happen is another illustration of how directly setting can impinge upon characterization.

Theme can also be directly affected by setting. The setting can become a central symbol or metaphor, not only unifying other aspects of the story but illuminating its central idea. Mark Twain's *Huckleberry Finn* is one obvious example that comes to mind. When Huck and Tom step onto their raft and set out down the Mississippi, their voyage becomes a story of life in microcosm. The river setting, so rich in religious and American symbolism, becomes more than a river, Huck's journey finally becoming a voyage into manhood—and life.

The writer's imagination can benefit from setting research. Very often, researching factual information for a story, or visiting an actual site to experience it physically, will fire her imagination in unexpected ways.

Perhaps you'll forgive another autobiographical illustration. When I visited California's Napa Valley several years ago, researching information about winemaking for use in the setting of my novel *The Winemakers*, I was quite concerned about how to open the novel in a way that would establish the setting and a sense of impending trouble at the same time. As I was walking through a winery with its owner one day, he cautioned me not to stumble over a number of heavy electrical cables on the concrete floor.

"Those control the temperature of the fermentation tanks," he explained. "If you pulled the plug, we could lose five hundred gallons of wine."

In that instant, my research into setting had set off my imagination and solved my problem with the opening of the book. If you read it today, you will find that it begins with a young winemaker arriving at her winery—and finding that someone has intentionally "pulled the plug."

TAKE YOUR TIME

Here we've looked at setting in a variety of ways, but in a cursory fashion. I hope I have managed to convince you that your handling of setting may be far more vital to your fiction project than you had previously suspected. In the chapters ahead we'll take a closer look at these and other aspects of setting, and how to maximize their potential in your story.

Let me urge you to work through the chapters slowly, seeking out ways you can reconsider your own work in light of the matters being discussed. It may help you to have copies of some of your own completed stories at hand as you study. As a point is made here, you may benefit by pausing to absorb the idea, and then carefully looking at some of your own copy to see if you have considered the idea in your past work. If not, you should ask yourself why not; if so, you should ask yourself if your new understanding might improve what you did earlier, perhaps without knowing why. If you choose to rewrite portions of your earlier material before moving on through this book, so much the better.

There's no tremendous hurry, you see, and hasty reading without action on your part might let important technical information go in one ear and right out the other. I encourage you to take your time and apply each chapter to your own work before moving on to the next.

After all, you remember the cliché—"Rome wasn't built in a day." *Your* story's Rome, if it's to be convincing, can't be built overnight either.

CHAPTER 2

PRESENTING SENSE IMPRESSIONS

WHEN MOST WRITERS THINK of the word "setting," they think of the physical impressions of the story world: the look, sound and smell of the place or places where the story takes place.

As we move along through this book, we'll also consider many other aspects of fiction which can rightfully be considered part of setting, but first let's consider the sense impressions of the story world.

Your use of description is vital in putting the reader into the story world. Use of vivid descriptions places him imaginatively inside the setting, transporting him to your story world through an appeal to his senses.

Sense impressions, therefore, are tremendously important in presenting your setting and keeping your reader intensely, physically aware of it. An in-depth examination of descriptive methodology is beyond the scope of this book, but we'll take a cursory look at some techniques in chapter fourteen. For now, a brief overview might help.

A truth every writer should keep in mind is that when she stops to describe something in fiction, the progress of the story usually stops while she does so. Fiction readers seek movement in their fiction, and so every "pause to describe" can be a dangerous one, threatening to weaken or even kill the reader's interest.

What is one to do, then, given the equally compelling truth that description of the story setting is vital to reader belief and physical involvement?

The answer is that descriptions generally should be kept to

a few words or a few lines at any given spot. Sensory descriptions should be sprinkled throughout the story, rather than "dumped" in great gobs. Handled this way, descriptive passages won't slow the story for long, and the reader will be reminded again and again — in short passages — how the story setting feels.

THE FIVE SENSES

Psychologists have repeatedly shown that sight is the dominant sense for most normal people. Therefore, it stands to reason that your sense descriptions most often will be dominated by how things appear. Hearing impressions usually rank second, but one can easily imagine circumstances in which tactile impressions might rank higher in story importance. So let's look briefly at each of the five senses you'll hope to touch in most of your stories.

Sight impressions may be of various kinds. There is a common misconception that one has covered the waterfront if she tells what colors can be seen in a given setting. Color is important, but — again according to psychological research findings — we know that a person's sight impressions of a given setting come into consciousness in a specific order.

Spatial dimension is often noted first. How large is the area? How open or closed? How high is the ceiling, if there is one? How far away is the sight-horizon if we're outdoors? How big or small does this space that we're describing feel to the onlooker?

The source of light is usually noted next or may be noticed simultaneously with dimension. Where does the light come from? How bright is it? Is it white light, or a mixture of subtle hues? (If we are "walking the reader" into a room, for example, is there a wall of high windows, or a single slit in a solid gray wall? And if a wall of windows, is the light that streams through sunny or cloudy gray?)

The dominant color of a setting may be striking and important. In describing a desert, for example, you may stress — after the vastness of the scene, and perhaps the glare — the monotonous tan of the terrain under a harsh, copper-colored sky.

Texture may also play a role in sight impression. The play of shadows over a weather-shattered cliff face may be a crucial sight impression; so might be the perfectly flat and placid surface of a small mountain lake on a windless day.

Contrasting shades of color are sometimes a dominant aspect of sight. The leaves of a tree might be green in actuality, for example, but in the context of your story they might look like sharply defined black shapes against the brilliance of the blue sky. That yellow fire truck might be more vibrant if it's seen parked in front of a red brick wall. Contrast often enlivens sight impression.

Hearing impressions are also crucial. The loudness of sound in a given setting is, of course, important, but also consider what is the tonality of the sound. Is it harsh or melodious? Why?

Is the sound a simple, single-source one, or a complex of many sounds? Should you transport your reader by concentrating on the single high wail of an ambulance siren, or would your setting be made more vivid if you depicted the siren sound almost lost in the groan of a garbage truck nearby, the honking of taxi horns, the roar of a diesel engine and the rumble of a subway beneath the pavement?

The identity and direction of a source of sound may be important. Is the sound coming from a distance, or close? Is it in the room or beyond the walls? Is it the muffled echo of a gunshot or the whimper of a child?

Assuming you are telling your story from the viewpoint of a character inside the action, that character's interpretation of the sound or sounds may also be highly significant in your description of it. For example, your character in the woods hears a low, guttural animal sound. Does she interpret it in terms of remembering how her pet dog used to grumble at squirrels, or does the image of a hungry grizzly instantly leap into her mind?

The sense of smell often ranks third in the hierarchy of sense impressions in a setting, usually far below sight and hearing because it is a more primitive sense, one we often tend to overlook or discount in real life. We often notice only strong odors, whether pleasant or unpleasant, and seldom form a strong judgment about a setting on the basis of them alone. Also, for most writers, describing odors is difficult and seldom seems highly relevant.

Yet, a woodland setting might come to life most vividly for the reader through a brief, cogent mention of the scent of pine and fallen leaves. The terror of a fire might come partly from the stinging cloud of smoke that threatens to choke bystanders. In such cases, an appeal to the sense of smell might be called for, or even demanded.

Tactile sensations—feeling with the fingertips or the surface of the skin—are more individualistic than most of the other senses mentioned thus far. Here we are dealing with physical feeling—roughness or smoothness, heat and cold, and the like. While there are imaginable circumstances in which the description of the setting through tactile sensations might be in order—in a story of someone threatened by freezing after being lost in a blizzard, for one obvious example—such sensations usually form a small part of the setting of a story.

Taste impressions, as part of setting, will be highly individualized. This sense is seldom used to a marked degree. But in those rare instances where a description of a taste—sweetness or bitterness, saltiness, acidity—may be called for, they too form a part of the physical setting of the tale.

As a fiction writer, you'll come upon occasions when you want to appeal to most of the senses in an attempt to make your story setting vivid and appealing. However, just as you must be accurate in factual background, you can't allow yourself to be "carried away" by some poetic flight of fancy in describing. Bluebirds *are* blue, and readers aren't going to like it if you change the color to orange because you think it might be more vivid.

HOW TO DELIVER SENSE IMPRESSIONS WITH PRECISION

It is not enough, though, to stick to known and verifiable impressions, and to sprinkle them in with care. Readers yearn for the most vivid and striking physical presentations of setting that you are capable of giving. Here, then, are some additional points that you should keep in mind.

If you know your story setting well, your notebook and imagination will be teeming with sense impressions you want to convey to the reader in order to make the story world vivid. But there is a danger that you might overdo it. The key here is to avoid generalizations or vagueness, and stick to specific, concrete detail.

Suppose, for example, you are trying to describe a fine country morning, and you bog down in generalizations and vague, catchall phrases (the words italicized in the following). You might come up with something like this:

> The *beautiful* day began with a *bright* sun in a *clear* sky and a *gentle* breeze moving through the *handsome* trees behind the *big* house. Beyond the *wide* river, through a *slight* veil of mist, the *buildings* of the *town* could be seen. . . .

Clearly, one might go on for pages with this kind of vague and generalized description, and never really get anywhere. If you search for a few words that are as specific and concrete as possible, however, you may achieve your story goals and get on with things in a hurry, as follows:

> Shading her eyes against the brilliant sun, Cassie squinted into the chilly breeze, trying to penetrate the smokelike haze over the river. Beyond it, the town's buildings jutted up like a child's blocks tumbled onto the ground.

We'll look more deeply at such questions of precision in wording in chapter fourteen. The point here is simply to start you thinking about the relationship between specificity of information and style. If you are specific enough, and strive to write with sharp impact, this in itself will tend to prevent your writing descriptive passages that are too long.

One further thought about "overkill" detail: Repetition of exactly the same sense impressions makes a story dull and predictable. Similarly, repetition of the same background facts can be deadly dull. If you need to repeatedly mention the frigid weather, for example, find a different way to refer to it each time. You can't simply keep saying it's cold outside. Instead, consider dropping in brief mentions of details like the following:

- the shrill wind against the roof shingles
- thick ice encrusting the inside of the windows
- a character's breath issuing from her lungs in steamy clouds
- brittle snowflakes swirling in the misty night
- a character shivering and wishing for a heavier coat
- a stray dog shaking miserably from the cold
- tingling pain in ears and fingers
- eyes watering from the chill wind
- smoke billowing densely from every chimney in sight
- the crunch of hard-frozen snow under a man's boots
- cold-reddened faces and hands
- low, thick snow clouds overhead

All of these small details will say "It's cold!" without ever saying it directly or in a repetitious manner.

In like fashion, suppose you need to say that the town which is your setting has a hostile feel about it—that the people distrust strangers. The reader is likely to get infuriated if you say this straight out more than once or twice. But, again, you can create any number of small details to show this trait of the setting in different words. (As a small exercise, you might wish to pause here and compose a list of possible setting details that would continually emphasize the town's hostile nature without boring repetition of the same words.)

With the selection of small but accurate details like these you can provide continual emphasis on setting without becoming repetitious. Use of this technique, along with cognizance of plot pressure to keep things moving along at a good pace, will put setting in its place as a critical but never obtrusive aspect of your storytelling.

THE VIEWPOINT

In order to be precise and convincing, you must be aware of another angle in your presentation of setting, and that's the viewpoint from which the sensory information is seen.

Beginning writers sometimes thoughtlessly assume an omniscient viewpoint—the see-everything and know-everything viewpoint of a godlike creator standing over the entire setting. Sometimes such a viewpoint is economical and the simplest way of putting down relatively large quantities of data in the smallest possible space.

Virtually all fiction, however, is told from a viewpoint, from the head and heart of a character inside the story action. Therefore, very often your job as a writer depicting some aspect of setting is to determine what the viewpoint character can realistically know or experience at any given moment—then to limit your presentation to that.

How can you know when to deliver information "from on high," and when from a character's viewpoint? The simplest answer might be found by following this three-point procedure:

1. Determine which impressions must be given "from on high" because (a) no character can see or experience them all, or (b) they can be given much more simply and vividly from outside a limited viewpoint.

2. Present descriptions "from on high" only at the beginning of story chapters or sections, when there has been a break in the time or action and you have not yet reestablished a character viewpoint since the break.

3. After establishing a viewpoint in any given section, present all further descriptions from inside that viewpoint, only as that viewpoint person could experience them.

Looking at each of these points in more detail:

As stated in No. 1, above, some sensory information cannot realistically be seen or known by any character inside the story. Suppose you wish to set up in the reader's mind the threat of a dam breaking and possibly flooding a town. If any character inside the story knew about this threat, he would surely sound an alarm. Therefore, in order to show the reader the cracks in the dam and the rising water pressure behind it, you have no choice but to get out of that limiting character viewpoint at the beginning of a chapter, say, and to present your description of the situation from an anonymous, godlike viewpoint. Then, having established knowledge of the setting threat in your reader's mind, you can enter the viewpoint of an innocent character inside the town.

Or, you might wish to portray a gathering storm. A story character *might* see this coming. But in order to alert the reader through a character viewpoint, you would have to drop in some references to clouds on the horizon, a freshening wind, the sound of distant thunder, or a drop in temperature to make the character aware of the storm so that the reader could become aware through that character's observations. Sometimes you might go through all this; other times it might be far more economical to adopt a godlike viewpoint and simply describe the gathering clouds and rising winds on a broader scale than anyone in the story could sense them.

Moving to No. 2, when you do choose to describe from an omniscient viewpoint, you should do so only at the beginning of story segments where no viewpoint for that segment has yet been established.

Why? Because readers like to get into a viewpoint, and once they do, they imaginatively experience everything in the story world from inside the character's head and heart. If you are in a chapter, say, and in character Joe's viewpoint, it's extremely jarring to the reader if you suddenly drop out of viewpoint and start describing things on a broader scale than Joe could possibly know.

Between sections or chapters, the reader tends to relax his viewpoint focus. After a break in the time or action, he'll more readily accept an omniscient passage. So this is the spot where you can most gently drop out of character viewpoint in order to present setting description from a broader perspective.

Note, however, the advice given in No. 3: Once you've established a character viewpoint in a given section, it's important to present all information from inside that viewpoint.

Perhaps two additional illustrations will further clarify these points. Both are from my novel, *Twister*, and in both cases my objective was to describe a part of the setting that was at the heart of the story: a storm spawning multiple tornadoes across more than half the United States. I wanted to describe what such a storm would be like to an individual trapped in it. But I also wanted to show "the big picture" that no single individual could experience. Therefore, I had to assume different vantage points.

One of the limited vantage points I chose was that of a farm woman named Milly, and my primary intention was to show how a tornado might be experienced by someone like her, in the storm's path. Therefore, the segment began in Milly's viewpoint as the tornado approached — this part of the dynamically changing setting being described as she would experience it, in viewpoint. I have italicized the words which establish or reinforce her restricted viewpoint:

> Out in front, not far across the road, a perfectly vertical column of blackness spun wildly. Its hollow interior was lighted by the strange bluish-white light that bathed everything else. The column seemed to be composed of rings of spinning clouds, one on top of the other like a stack of pale tires, and *as Milly watched, she saw* one ring near the bottom work its way upward, seeming to slip over others above it until it was out of view. Boards and small trees and other unrecognizable objects hurled around and around in the rotating column. *She saw* a small tree fly out of the column and flop to the ground like a killed fish. The sound was either *too great for Milly's ears*, or they had been broken by *the intense pain she felt in them*. . . .

There is nothing here that Milly cannot logically and credibly experience. (You may also notice that shape, light and movement are described first, with hearing noted at the end.) This passage achieved the goal set out for it, describing a single person's experience of this part of the setting.

A chapter or two later, however, my intention was to show

a broader view of a storm approaching a town. In this case, no single individual could possibly know everything I wanted to tell, nor could any single character see the panorama I wished the reader to experience. Therefore, the following passage opened a segment after a time-and-space transition clearly marked by extra white spaces in the text:

> The Thatcher tornado, one of three suspended under a single enormous thundercloud cell some nine miles in diameter and towering more than seventy thousand feet in altitude, was at its peak of life as it reached the southwest edge of Southtown, on a northeasterly path that would take it through the heart of the city. It was one mile wide at its mouth, with winds of two hundred miles per hour crushing, smashing and destroying everything in its range, and could not be seen as a classic twister, but rather as a gigantic ebony obscuration from ground to sky, swirling, shrieking with a sound like none other in the world. . . .

Thus you make your viewpoint decisions based on your intent at the moment in the story, and you place them in the most advantageous structural locations. There will be more about these decisions in later chapters, as the need to discuss them arises.

A FINAL WORD ON THE SENSES

Before closing this look at sensory description, one point should be emphasized yet again, and that has simply to do with accuracy. However hard you strive to be vivid, or whatever device you may choose to put the reader into your physical story setting, please remember that you must never deviate from verifiable facts. A single slip — describing a certain known flower by the wrong color, for example — might so offend your reader that many of your subsequent descriptions might be met with skepticism, or worse. *Never* deviate from the factual in your physical descriptions.

Accuracy! It's so important.

In the next chapter we'll look at another aspect of setting where accuracy is also supremely important, one closely related to what we have been discussing here. That involves setting information based less on physical senses and more on hard, cold fact.

Which doesn't have to be cold at all, as we shall see.

CHAPTER 3

PRESENTING FACTUAL MATERIAL

FACTUAL BACKGROUND IS OFTEN AS ESSENTIAL to a story as its physical look and feeling. Thus one of your major jobs as a writer is to know how to handle the presentation of facts in your fiction.

Some aspects of factual background may be simple, such as knowing what kind of weather to portray in west Texas in August. Others may become more esoteric, such as knowing how many strands of barbed wire a rancher would realistically string in your western novel set in the year 1875. And still others might be more demanding yet, such as the need to portray with great accuracy the facts of a surgical procedure being done in your medical novel. Whatever factual material you choose to present as part of your story fabric, it must first of all be right.

ACCURACY

It's disturbing to me how often fiction writers say that they don't have to worry much about factual information in their setting because "I made the town up," or "I never specify exactly where or when it is." Such ideas don't hold water. Factual data about the setting must always be as accurate as practicality allows.

For example, even if you're presenting a fictional town in an unnamed region, there must be an internal factual consistency about the setting. The town should at least be identifiable as being in the South, let's say, or in the Rocky Mountains. Within

19

this general frame of reference, you must be factually accurate.

By way of illustration: In the southern setting you might show crape myrtles in bloom, but you'd better know they bloom late in the summer, and usually have pink or orchid-colored flowers, or they might also be white. In the high mountains, crape myrtles winter-kill; there you may have lilacs — but in the spring. Similarly, it might be possible for your imaginary town to have a snowstorm in June if it were set in northern Montana, but if your general reference area were in the South, such a snow would require a lot more explaining!

Thus even a very vague story setting requires general factual accuracy. And most story settings are much more specific and require far greater attention to factual detail. You as a fiction writer must always remember this principle: even a single factual error in your setting may destroy all credibility for your story . . . all reader belief.

One example: Several years ago, there was a novel (whose title and author have long since escaped me) with a plot about the abduction of the president of the United States in his Air Force One. Much was made in promotion copy and advertising about the research the novelist had done to make the aircraft setting accurate. This might have been quite true. But in reading the novel, I noticed a careless and fundamental error: The author had thoughtlessly guessed about the transmitting range of a communications device on the plane, and he worked out a key aspect of his plot by making a tiny radio transmit farther than it ever really could have done. This error, small as it was in terms of the total factual background in the novel, was so crucial that it destroyed all my faith in the accuracy of the rest of the background — and I was not the only reader who noticed; reviewers did, too, and the novel was not successful partly because this single bad mistake had wrecked its air of verisimilitude.

I once encountered a more serious factual error in setting when a young woman brought me a novel set in Saudi Arabia. She had carefully researched that Arab nation, and her story brimmed with fascinating facts about the country as well as vivid descriptions of exotic sights. Unfortunately, she had overlooked one crippling fundamental error. The whole plot of her book was based on the idea of a young woman visiting Saudi Arabia as a tourist. The author had not uncovered the fact that Saudi Arabia does not allow tourists to enter the country. Thus the novel was factually impossible.

Never assume you know something if you haven't checked it out. I used to test writing students by giving them a number of statements to complete which in reality could have only one outcome. One such statement said the character "shoved the throttle of the plane fully forward." More than half my students, year after year, wrote for a result that "the engine died" or "the motor slowed" or some such, thoughtlessly assuming that the throttle of an airplane must work the same way as a throttle on an old car or a tractor, where pushing the knob forward decreases power. Unfortunately for all those who guessed on the basis of such an analogy, an aircraft throttle works the opposite; you push forward for more power, not less. The correct factual response had to be that the engine roared, the plane's altitude or speed changed, or something close to that.

Once more: Never assume you know a fact about setting if you haven't checked it out. All stated facts about the setting must be accurate if the story is to be believed.

The weather in a given place at a given time of year should, as already mentioned, be in line with actuality. Further, if you happen to be writing about a specific place and a specific actual date, I would advise you to go so far as to check old newspapers or almanacs to find out what the weather really was at that time, in that place. (I thoughtlessly assumed once that a quite ordinary day in June of a certain year was warm and windy in Montana. I received two letters from outraged readers pointing out that I had failed to take note that *that* June period saw the biggest early-summer snowstorm in state history. I have decided you can't be too careful about anything.)

Many readers won't know if you guess, but a surprising number will check up on you . . . and immediately lose all belief in the rest of your story after they find one verifiable error. More dangerous to you as a writer is the fact that if you guess about one seemingly minor thing, you may fall into the habit of guessing about things that many readers may notice, to your everlasting discredit and unpopularity.

Know the kinds of trees and shrubs and animals that should be shown in the area you depict. Know the feel of the place, whether the typical day is sun-washed and brilliant or gray and grungy. Know the ethnic composition of the neighborhood, and how the people talk. Know clothing styles, characteristic shelter and transportation. Know what things cost. Know the local slang and what people are most concerned about.

Did you know, for example (as I learned in my student's doomed novel about Saudi Arabia), that Saudi citizens' idea of an entertaining time is to go out into the scrubland and build a big fire and roast meat on a spit? This current setting fact goes back to the history of the setting, that of a nomadic culture. Or did you know that a Saudi man is allowed four wives—but is obliged to treat all equally, so that if one wife gets a house, all wives must have an equal house, and so on? Again, this cultural/religious rule goes back to the region's history and long-standing traditions, which are a vital part of the general setting. And you have to get them right.

WHEN IS TOO MUCH "TOO MUCH"?

Readers today are better informed than any in history. They receive more information from more sources than readers did even a decade ago, and they tend to want more information in their fiction. In the current information revolution, some of them actually seem to feel guilty about reading fiction unless they can convince themselves that they are also learning something. Therefore, recognizing this trend in readership generally, novelists tend to pack much more hard information into their story settings. If you look for solid data in most novels today—even "frothy" ones—you may be surprised to see how much hard research went into them.

But does this mean there is no practical limit to how much hard fact you should provide? By no means. You must not simply pile page after page of fact onto your setting scaffold. Rather,

you should have a rich lode of factual information on hand before you begin to write, and should know how to sprinkle in
those facts a few at a time in places where they will best fit into
the flow of your narrative. Note that both parts of the equation
are necessary in providing readers with sufficient factual data
about your setting: having plenty of accurate information, and
knowing how to sprinkle it in, a bit at a time, at the right times.

A point is made of this duality of purpose because there are
writers who err by ignoring one part or the other. Some research heavily and gather fascinating details, then succumb to
the temptation to dump it all, in long, boring imbedded essays
which stop the story, shift the focus from characters to
encyclopedia-type data, irritate the reader, and finally put him
to sleep. Other writers, knowing they can't shovel in loads of
facts, respond by not gathering many facts to begin with—or by
carelessly guessing at a few. Either course is disastrous.

You can never have too much factual information on hand
about your setting. You will often be amazed by how much you
manage to work in, a dribble at a time. But even if some of it
never gets into your story, your knowledge of this information
will enrich your storytelling because you the author will know
the story world in all its details as well as, or better than, any
character.

How do you know how much setting information to insert
into your narrative at any given time? Unfortunately, this is
largely a matter of "feel," and you can never be entirely sure.
But one aspect of fiction that will help you decide when "enough
is enough" is plot pressure. If your story's plot is "working,"
your characters should be under some pressure—both in terms
of story time and emotion—virtually throughout. If you have
your plot working in this way, you simply may not have time to
dump in too many facts, nor will your characters have time to
notice or discuss too many facts at any given moment.

What am I implying here? Simply this: If you find yourself
stopping the story action again and again to drop in lengthy
information about the setting, this may be a clue to you that your
plot is not "tight" enough—is not putting enough immediate
pressure on the characters. Often you can answer the question

of how much setting information to put in at any given point by looking at the pressure on the characters — and increasing that immediate pressure if you find that you have nothing going on which would realistically preclude someone thinking quietly about their hometown's demographics for half a chapter, or reciting other facts to some other story person.

So if you suspect that you're putting in undesirable gobs of uninterrupted factual information (or excessive sensory description, for that matter), look at your plot. Try to devise ways to make things tougher on your story people so that there simply will not be time for overindulgence in setting details.

PROBLEM SITUATIONS

But what about the times when you may have detailed factual data or story information that you want your viewpoint character to learn in the course of the story? In such cases, clearly, you need to have the information given to the character in his viewpoint. So what do you do? Have someone walk up to the character in the story and start pointing things out to him, and telling him facts?

I hope not. When you want your viewpoint character to observe certain things or learn certain facts, you must not have some other character simply dump the information on his head. What you need to do, rather, is to create inside your viewpoint character a need and desire to notice something or learn certain things. Then you can have him set out to reconnoiter a mountainside, for example, or interrogate some other character.

Having set up a felt need for certain setting information inside your viewpoint character, you can realistically have him go off in search of it. In this way, you set up a little sub-quest in the plot — the character seeking information about the setting and situation.

Following are two examples of such a situation where the author has decided that a character needs certain information. The first is a clumsy and horrid example of how *not* to do it.

Ralph walked into the bar. He did not know it, but it was the same bar where his brother Jake had been seen two weeks earlier.

The bartender came over and squinted at Ralph. "You look familiar," he said.

"I do?" Ralph said.

"You look a lot like a man who was in here two weeks ago. He said his name was Jake. He looked tired that evening . . . said he was going to register at the Zuider Zee Motel down the street. That's the one the police raided the other night, you know. The police chief—his name is Sam Spade—believed there was gambling going on there. But back to this man Jake. I asked him where he came from, and. . . ."

This is pretty bad. The "He did not know it" line at the top is a clear violation of viewpoint, the author clumsily stepping in to say something the character does *not* know, then using another character to dump information on Ralph (and the reader) in a totally unbelievable way.

How much better it works if we have set up Ralph's need to learn information in the bar, perhaps as follows.

Ralph found the bar where his brother had been seen two weeks earlier. Somehow, he thought, he had to learn why Jake had come here, from where, and—most important—where he had planned to go next.

The bartender seemed surly. Ralph ordered a beer, and then tried to collect information.

"Are you the regular man on duty at this time?" he asked.

"That's me," the bartender said. "Why?"

"Would you have been working two weeks ago tonight?"

"Say, fella, what is this? Twenty questions?"

"I'm trying to locate my brother. His name is Jake Wheelan. He was in this bar two weeks ago tonight. I thought you might have seen him. He and I look a lot alike."

The bartender frowned and leaned closer. "I might

have seen him, at that. What is it exactly you want to know?"

"Well, first. . . ."

As this example makes clear, sometimes you can get important information into your story without having to retreat to an "on-high" vantage point. Your viewpoint character can ask questions, and you can get the information into the story that way—both for the reader's use and as motivation of your character.

On the other hand, there will be cases when you must have the wisdom to take a broader view. Suppose you are writing a historical novel which looks at a small section of the country and how it is about to be engulfed in a freshet of immigration. From an omniscient, "on-high" point of view, you can tell the reader about national business setbacks, the influx of immigrants from Europe to the East Coast, even the lingering aftereffects of a recent war. You can paint a much broader canvas than any character inside the story could possibly portray for you.

At this point we need only remember that there are such viewpoint choices—and they are yours to make wisely, with thought. There are a number of other things to consider in choosing and showing viewpoint, but it's necessary to look at some other matters before we go deeper into that. We'll return to the subject in chapter ten, with other aspects considered in the chapter following that.

START THINKING "RESEARCH"

In the meantime, work on your own habits as they relate to accuracy in the presentation of facts in your setting. This will mean research. (One can't always write about the hometown neighborhood she already knows intimately.) Appendix 1, starting on page 155, looks at research methods and procedures, and you should begin dipping into it as soon and as often as necessary.

Start getting more familiar with your local library and bookstores. By all means, browse them! Allot an hour or two, or more, on a regular basis. Stroll past the shelves. Acquaint yourself with the kinds of factual information available. Notice, for example, that travel books deal mostly with physical matters, and can be invaluable to you in learning how to describe a setting, but you may unearth equally crucial information about history or custom or regional attitudes in books to be found in the history section, or in an area devoted to social sciences. The more you browse, the more resources you'll uncover.

Before you go on, however, perhaps this chapter has suggested something you need to look at again in some of your own copy? Is there a fact to recheck . . . or a better way to present your factual material?

Take your time.

CHAPTER 4

FUDGING FACTS: WHEN IT'S OKAY TO STRAY FROM TRUTH

HAVING WORKED HARD TO CONVINCE you of the need for absolute accuracy in setting, I am now forced to confront you with a paradoxical statement:

There are occasions in fiction when *inaccuracy* may be beneficial—when a writer can score considerable gains for herself by deviating from actuality either by bending the facts or making some up.

A number of reasons exist for this.

As we shall explore in chapter five, readers of certain fiction genres expect and virtually demand qualities of setting which may be more mythological than real. Woe be to the unwary writer who deviates from such genre-reader expectations, regardless of actuality!

We'll discuss the matter further in that later chapter, but one example might be mentioned here for clarification. Readers of traditional western adventure stories generally expect the tale to take place in "the warm West," which means that most westerns take place in the heat of summer, and usually in semiarid areas such as west Kansas or Texas. Horsemanship is almost always some part of the setting, and so are firearms and gunplay. The setting almost always includes philosophical ideals of manly courage, independence and quick justice, and the cowboy and land baron, rough as they might be, were building an empire, please remember, not raping an environment!

All such reader expectations about a story's setting may require you to deviate considerably from the actual truth.

ARTISTIC LICENSE

Are there other instances when you can safely deviate from the facts about setting? Yes. Here are some examples of what you can do.

Invent a town or area, within reason. Your story situation may make it necessary to invent a town or area rather than placing your story precisely in an actual one. Most of the reasons you would do this are mundanely practical. You don't have access to every small physical detail of the real town in Bavaria you want to portray, for example, but you have general memories of the area, and access to guidebooks which show pictures of several towns similar to the one you vaguely remember. In such a case, making up your own town might keep you true to the spirit and feeling of a real place, but free you from worry that you might get a street name wrong or a bit of history garbled. Or you might be basing your story loosely on actual events — a murder, say, or grand theft that really took place. Placing your story in the actual town where the crime was committed would lead every person in the real town to look for themselves in your story, and thus naming the actual town might open you up to misidentifications (or real ones!) — and lawsuits. Far better in such circumstances to make up your own town, similar to the real one.

Invention of a town or area as setting may free you creatively and legally, too. But a proviso must be added, and that is this: The invented place must be true to the general area and time in which you invent it. It simply won't work to set a story in 1976 and have your railroad line using mostly steam locomotives; these were generally phased out of use in favor of diesel power in the 1950s. Similarly, just because you happen to make up your particular small town in upper New York state, you can't have everybody speaking in an accent or with slang totally out of keeping with that general geographical area — then plead that you can do whatever you want because the town is imaginary. The rules of credibility apply even in a wholly fictional setting, and most writers who make up a town pattern it closely after a real, known one — or well-researched one — in order to avoid gaffes like having considerable oil drilling taking place in modern-day Oklahoma, where the oil business has declined radically in recent years, or putting a mountain anywhere near Oklahoma City.

Put actual historical (or contemporary) personages in your fiction. Writers often worry greatly about when they can and cannot put real people in their story settings and plots. A rule that perhaps errs on the side of safety is that you can put actual people in cameo roles. It's a fairly popular device, one I've used myself in a series of novels about an international tennis player I call Brad Smith. There is no Brad Smith, and he is made out of whole cloth. But as part of the story setting, any number of actual tennis stars, from Bjorn Borg to Chrissie Evert, show up in cameo speaking roles.

Such a setting device tends to add verisimilitude to the yarn and to make the reader believe in the wholly fictional characters. Generally there is nothing wrong with this, even though making up dialogue for real people, and even minor actions in the plot, is clearly a departure from reality. Again, however, you shouldn't stray too far from the truth: If you put Jimmy Connors on the tennis court in your story, you can't make him right-handed; readers will notice that and chalk it up to your ignorance, thus diminishing your credibility as a storyteller.

The legal ramifications of using real people in your fiction are not complicated. The basics have not changed in over a half-century. In both civil and criminal libel, three elements must be present to establish libel has taken place. The words used must be defamatory; they must be published; and the person libeled must be identified. (Fredrick Siebert, J.D.: *The Rights and Privileges of the Press*; Appleton-Century Co., 1934.)

Beyond this, courts have generally held that the alleged libel must have been written and published "willfully." That is to say, the offended party must prove that the accused writer meant to do harm. This is a very difficult allegation to prove, as many failed libel suits have proven. However, all writers should remember that there have been rare cases where a judge ruled that the writer printed a damaging falsehood, and should have been more careful. In such cases, a "reckless disregard for the truth"—the terminology often used in journalism school lecture halls—may be interpreted as proof of an indifference to fact so sloppy and brazen that the resulting falsehood can be considered "willful."

Also remember that truth is its own defense. If you are sued for libel and can absolutely prove the veracity of what you wrote, you cannot be found guilty of libel. (Of course you might go through a great deal of emotional torment and expense before you are vindicated in a court of law.)

Public figures such as elected officials are almost impossible to libel when the writer is writing about official duties. All such comment, including newspaper editorials, is considered "fair comment."

The published material must bring the subject person into disrepute and actually damage his or her reputation, and you can't libel the dead.

Beyond these basic points lies a swamp of legal nit-picking. Great, fat books have been written on libel. Occasionally a court renders a libel ruling which subtly alters the body of "case law," creating some new precedent every subsequent judge may have to consider in rendering a verdict, but all of these fine points take us far beyond the scope of this chapter.

In addition to libel laws, the writer must be concerned about laws protecting citizens' right to privacy. These are far broader and less specific. If you put a real person in your story, and if he or she doesn't happen to like your portrayal, you might find yourself sued for invasion of that person's privacy.

Such cases might be filed virtually by anyone on any pretext, and there are a lot of people out there eagerly looking for a chance to sue somebody and make some easy money. A writing friend of mine was once sued for millions by the family of a dead official with a shady past. The story mentioned some of the dead man's alleged shady dealings. The family sued for invasion of their privacy by the writer's mentioning the dead man's chicanery, and while they ended up losing their case, my friend spent more than two years in agony as the case dragged on, to his considerable expense in legal fees.

The moral here is that you should be extremely careful in

matters involving real people, living or dead. That rule—and the always-present need for the greatest possible verisimilitude in your stories—guides all the observations that follow here.

My own rule is to use real people only in harmless cameo roles, and to reduce even the use of actual historical personages to a safe minimum. I generally make up my specific locales—at least the restricted area of a known city or state my story may play in—and use real people supersafely.

An actual example might further illustrate the last two points about making up a town and putting real people in cameo roles. In his novel *The Night Hunters*, mystery writer John Miles opens with a prologue that begins as follows.

In the summer of 1962, the President of the United States flew 2,000 miles in order to cut a ribbon and open twelve miles of two-lane asphalt highway. The new road followed the ridged crest of a wooded hill system—steps to the Ozarks—in the most desolate and beautiful section of southeastern Oklahoma.

The President's aides spoke of his abiding interest in projects designed to preserve natural beauty and stimulate pride in the nation, and the President himself, standing tall and young with the brisk Oklahoma wind in his sandy hair, spoke movingly of our heritage. . . .

It was by all odds the biggest day in the history of the town of Noble in Archer County, Oklahoma. . . .

This segment combines historical and geographical fact with invention. It is a fact that John Kennedy went to Oklahoma in 1962 to dedicate a short stretch of scenic highway. But the town most directly affected was not Noble, but Big Cedar. Newspaper accounts do not reflect remarks by the president that day about "our heritage," but about development of natural resources. Further, there is no "Archer County" in Oklahoma, and although there is a real town of Noble, it is located in Cleveland County, faraway from the story locale, in the middle of the state.

Miles's deviations from actuality were not the type that readers would "jump on" as inaccurate. Clearly, he was taking liberties with actuality in order to lay out the background setting for a story to be played out in and around a fictional town in a fictional county—much like a real town in a real county.

The plot of Miles's novel has to do with a hidden story involving a plot against the president's life on that visit long ago, and the long-hidden aftereffects of that murderous scheme. Far better to make up a town and some character dialogue so that the main plot might be believed, than to try to put the story in the actual town of Big Cedar, Oklahoma, where many readers would know that such a series of events never, ever, took place.

Invent dialogue for real people, even historical personages. What you can't do is try to prettify your setting by having actual persons, contemporary or historical, saying things clearly contrary to everything actually known about them. This is not a legal question but one of simple accuracy and verisimilitude. In a historical novel about Lewis and Clark, for example, you might reasonably show the two explorers discussing the wildlife and day's activities; you could extrapolate conversations like this from expedition journals, and possibly even allude to real past events. On the other hand, it might be going a bit too far to have Lewis telling Clark how frightened he is out here in the wilderness without his night light.

Change the location or timing of real events. You can also mildly alter other established facts, if the changes are not glaringly wrong. In one of my Brad Smith novels, for example, I changed the venue of events leading up to the Wimbledon tournament, making up a couple of warm-up tourneys that don't actually exist, and changing the dates for some others. Why? The different timing and placement of these parts of my fictional setting made my plot work better and more smoothly. In addition, had I used real locations in all cases, I would have had to spend another $10,000 visiting all such locales and tournaments in Great Britain in order to make sure I had every detail about the actual place perfectly accurate. In another Brad Smith book, set around Lake City, Colorado, I sent a car chase south of town and onto a creek-canyon road that does not really exist. Two other creek-canyon roads do exist south of town, but neither exactly fit my needs for the chase.

I don't think anyone objects very strenuously to changes

like these. In both cases, the deviations from actuality remained true to the kind and spirit of the real setting. Only details were altered for convenience.

Invent period jargon or slang. You can even write in such a way as to "fake" the sound of a period. This is especially true in historical fiction. It may be quite impossible to know exactly how the common person spoke in the England of 1700, for example. But writers depict the period setting's language peculiarities and cadences all the time. Sometimes, as more than one novelist has admitted, certain slang expressions were simply made up because they "sounded right," true to the cadence and feel of journals and other written documents of the time. Similarly, writers of science fiction often invent pseudotechnical doublespeak for characters to spout as part of the general technological setting of the story. But again, common sense must prevail. You simply can't have an Elizabethan character saying words like "groovy" or "okay," or starting sentences with the contemporary misusage, "Hopefully. . . ."

Imagine the clearly impossible. The setting of Michael Crichton's *Jurassic Park* is a theme park where prehistoric animals have been returned to life. My own novel *Ariel* was set in a computer lab featuring a large mainframe computer which began making its own telephone calls, and then "came to life." The key to making all such improbable or impossible settings work for the reader lies in making the impossible imaginable and acceptable—making the setting enough *like* something that *does* exist so that the reader can "buy it." The copious use of actual facts in presenting the setting is mandatory to get the reader to suspend disbelief. Crichton, for example, provides heavy detail on real scentific developments in biological engineering—cloning, and the like. I heavily researched work in artificial intelligence, computer design and childhood-learning theory before writing *Ariel*, and put heavy doses of facts about such real aspects of science in the novel as part of its setting.

The moral of this, perhaps, is that even when you make something up out of whole cloth—or perhaps especially when you do so—it's even more crucial that you know what the real facts are and present many of them to make your departure from actuality more credible. There seems to be no escaping the need for careful attention to detail—and research.

In all the cases mentioned in this chapter, the use of a vivid bit of setting that never really existed might be better than use of the real thing, even if scrupulously researched. But in every case we have seen the need for factual information lying behind the make-believe, as a point from which it can take off and still be believed. There are advantages, sometimes, in making up part of your setting, but that doesn't relieve you of the need to be accurate and true.

The trick, it seems to me, lies in seeing what might ring false to your reader—and never taking a chance in such a case. If you can construct part of your setting from memory of a real place, or from your imagination, it can be perfectly all right as long as you don't stray too far from what the reader knows is real. You can set your story in the fictional town of Bickham, nineteen miles outside of Houston, for example, and if you do so, you can make up street names and everything else since the town does not really exist. But you can't have a blizzard in August in that general locale, and if you have a character drive to Houston to shop, you'll have to have the street names and all other details of the real city accurate in every detail.

So, you can see that accuracy is a prime requisite even in an imagined setting. Imagined setting must be just as consistent and detailed as one built on an actual place or time. It cannot deviate from realities about the region or era. You may, for reasons of convenience or legality, obscure the actual identity of a place, or you may play loose with certain aspects of an actual place's history. You can make up a setting from memory or imagination. But your job always is to convince the reader. Specific detail is convincing, and generality is not. That's why made-up details of a setting are so often extrapolations, not wild invention, and why writers so often research heavily into a real setting before making up a similar one of their own; they want to have a lot of detail, and they want to be very close to what's really "out there" someplace.

A "DEPARTURE CHECKLIST"

Assuming you are considering making up part of your setting or deviating from actuality in some ways as you depict an actual setting, here are a few questions you might want to bear in mind — a sort of safety checklist for your departure from reality.

1. "Do I have good reason not to use the actual place or time?" If the only reason you're making up a setting is to make it easier on yourself, you may be making a mistake. You'll probably end up researching a real place, and then basing your imagined setting on hard facts, anyway.

2. "Am I sure that my imagined setting will be more vivid and believable than the actual place might be?" As useful as imagined settings may be, credibility is gained by placing your story in an actual, recognizable place and time. Don't carelessly assume that a made-up town, for example, would necessarily be more interesting than a real one you know well.

3. "Is my imagined setting close enough to a real one to be believed?" In other words, is your imagined setting credible? Are the details close enough to an actual place to be accepted without question by the reader?

4. "Do any of my imagined details fly in the face of reality?" Are you sure the weather is right for your region, for example, and if you are using real people in cameo roles, are you absolutely certain you have basic details about the real people perfectly correct?

5. "Do I have enough detail to be convincing?" Have you thought deeply enough about every aspect of your setting? Do you know everything you possibly could about it? Do you have mental or, preferably, actual drawn maps, for example, as well as biographies, dates and descriptions of places in your imagined history? Are there vague spots in your planning which must still be filled?

THE VALUE OF BUILDING FILES

Clearly, even if you don't fear the harrassment of lawsuits, you will want to make your story settings and people as credible as possible. To that end, for professional pride, if nothing else, you should start setting up some files, whether you intend to work primarily with actual settings or imagined ones. In either case you'll need background facts.

These files may be very general, with headings such as "Science," "Homes," "Rivers and Lakes," "Historic Romances," or whatever. As you read newspapers and magazines, be alert for material that might go into one of these files, or into a new one. I don't want you to become a file clerk, but a growing store of factual data for possible use in future story settings can become a priceless resource.

Even if you deviate far from actual places, persons and times, you need the background actuality as a support for your imaginings. As you move along in your fiction-writing career, you will find that you are building more and more of these files. This is all to the good because it will make your future work on settings easier. Most of us who have been in the business for a while have file drawers full of all manner of factual information that might be useful in a setting someday. Some of the clippings in my files go back many years and have never proven useful as yet, but I keep them because one never knows what strange byway his imagination may take.

CHAPTER 5

SETTING IN SPECIALIZED STORIES

As mentioned in the last chapter, readers come to certain genres — types of stories — expecting certain kinds of settings, certain details, certain intensities and lengths of description. In the example used earlier, it was noted that readers of traditional westerns expect — and even demand — that the setting have certain prototypical aspects.

This was brought out to me most forcefully early in my writing career when I myself was writing westerns. I wrote a novel set in a Colorado town in the middle of a severe winter when an avalanche cut the area off from all outside assistance. Although seemingly acceptable in every other regard, the manuscript was rejected several times on the basis, as one editor put it, that the story setting "lacks the traditional feeling of the warm West."

Since that time, the importance of meeting reader expectations about setting in certain genres has been brought home to me again and again. It's an aspect of setting seldom addressed by the experts, but it's very real. You, as a writer interested in improving your handling of setting, should be aware of how various genres bring with them built-in expectations about the setting that should be used.

The late Clifton Adams, one of the best western writers who ever lived, told me that the advantage of the traditional western setting lay in the fact that "The police won't come in and break up your fight just when you've got it going full-blast." That's one of the hard-core, practical reasons why most westerns take place in isolated settings — no one will break up the fight or jail the bad guys or rescue the hero from his plight.

Another reason for the isolation so typical of the western novel setting, however, is simply this matter of reader expectation. From the time of James Fenimore Cooper's tales of the early frontier, readers of western adventure have expected an isolated setting. Such readers aren't aware of the practical plotting advantages such a setting provides for the action writer; it's simply what these readers are used to, and it's what they want to find again in every new novel of the type that they read.

There are other aspects of setting that fit the western genre, too. Some were mentioned in chapter four. But there is also the matter of expansiveness . . . grand vistas . . . vast, open country. This sort of physical setting and open *feeling* is characteristic of nearly all such books.

The kind of people found as part of the setting in westerns is usually predictable, too. Sympathetic female characters, until the most recent time, were quiet, loyal, long-suffering and hard-working characters whose main function was to serve as romantic interest for the more-important males in the story, or to act as mirrors whose adoration made the men look more heroic. That's changed a bit in recent years, and today you can occasionally find a female in a western who is her own person and has some spunk. But the background cast of most westerns is male to this day, the masculine ethic forming part of the story's setting.

The males tend to form a story backdrop based on traditional values, including the work ethic, belief that right makes might (and not the opposite), and the heroic ideal of a lone man against heavy odds for the sake of justice. While the real West might have had a great number of strong and admirable black men, they seldom appear as part of the setting in a traditional western. And while in truth more men might have been shot in the back with a shotgun than killed in street duels, the setting of a western still often depends in part on the unexamined assumption that Marshal Dillon really did stride out into the middle of the street and outdraw a bad guy every once in a while. In the real West, six-guns misfired with dismaying regularity; in the traditional western, six-guns are as reliable as the finest modern weapon. In the real West, the women who made it as far as the frontier towns tended to be a bit on the tough, gnarled side. In the traditional western setting, they're more likely to resemble Michelle Pfeiffer. And so it goes.

The point here is not to disparage the western or any of the other genres we're going to examine. The point is that you as a writer should be aware of what your genre reader expects, and then remember that it is incumbent upon you to deliver the goods expected, whether they're in line with actual fact or not. Thus, in writing genre fiction, you have to be accurate in terms of the reader's expectation or the myth of the genre, rather than the actual truth.

Knowing your genres, then, will tell you where "accuracy" is located.

So let's briefly consider a few others.

ROMANCE

Readers of romance often turn to this genre for escape from the humdrum, relief from grim reality, and reassurance that life can be both beautiful and romantic—that dreams do indeed come true. What do these expectations say about romance settings?

Perhaps above all else, the romance depends on a philosophical setting—a group of beliefs assumed as true by the people in the story—based on the ideal of romantic love. The heroine may indeed be a young career woman quite capable of taking care of herself, and may even speak against "silly romantic love." But she is proven quite capable of being "swept off her feet." A belief in love-at-first-sight, so celebrated in popular songs, is essential to such a story; it is the bedrock belief-setting on which everything else is built.

Further—and bearing in mind that there are exceptions to every generalization—most romances play out in a physical setting which is in some way exotic or faraway or sharply different from the assumed reader's everyday world. Warm, flower-filled Caribbean islands were once the most popular setting, with small European kingdoms (peopled by princes and wealthy heirs) a close second. When these settings were used in too many novels, Central and South America came in for considerable play. There was a brief vogue for the hot Southwest, and Hawaii, and some romances continue to take place in mountain settings, including ski resorts. An occasional useful setting is the large city, but when such a setting is used, the author usually tries to make it out of the ordinary and exciting by stressing fabulous restaurants and clubs, great mansions of the rich and powerful, or the inner workings of some presumably intriguing business firm, a law office, perhaps, or bank.

What all these settings have in common is concrete detail in abundance showing a lifestyle environment far from that known in the everyday life of the average romance reader. Thus the physical setting provides a voyage of escape into an imagined world rich in wish fulfillment.

Because these escape settings form such an important part of the appeal of such stories, they are often written with a loose plot structure that puts relatively slight immediate time pressure on the characters, which in turn allows the author to dwell lovingly and at length on her descriptions of the setting or settings. Because the characters are not pressed to take immediate action in the plot, they have time to notice details of the setting, and the author can credibly devote lengthy passages to description while the characters presumably are doing little if anything.

This softness of plot tension in romances and its resulting opportunity for lengthy descriptions of the setting tend, in turn, to encourage a writing style which is comparatively loose, discursive, heavily ornamented and sensuous. When setting details are described from inside a viewpoint, such descriptions are often tied directly to strong emotional response in the character, so that further coloration of the prose results.

The total effect: Stories in which physical detail is heavily, even sumptuously described, and in which plot tension is usually slight in order to allow for such handling of setting. Thus, if you intend to write romance, you must not only observe acutely for colorful, exotic setting detail, you must also cultivate a full and rich prose style, and you should be careful not to create plot situations which put too much immediate pressure on the characters. For these elements — setting, style and plot — as different as they might appear on the surface, are inextricably tied together in the romance.

SUSPENSE

Readers of suspense fiction bring quite different expectations to this genre. Here the basic appeal is usually either intellectual puzzle (the mystery) or dire physical threat (the classic tale of espionage). While such stories may be very specialized, demanding a deeply researched and meticulously presented setting involving technology or the expertise of a specialized field, the background is not the primary reason why people read them. Here the plot and perhaps the characters are the thing.

What does this imply for you if you want to handle setting properly in such a genre? Three things:

1. The physical detail you present should be described briefly.
2. Your style should be crisp and understated.
3. The emotional background of the story—the tone of the piece—should be as chill as the romance is warm.

Physical detail should be shown briefly for two reasons: The reader of this genre is more interested in plot, and the plot usually will be so pressure-packed and suspenseful that neither character nor author can be involved for long periods of time (or long paragraphs on the page) in setting descriptions. This generalization is violated in novels such as "techno-thrillers," where heavily researched, in-depth factual or physical detail are a considerable part of the writer's appeal. But unless you are writing such a tome crammed with often-esoteric "inside information," the rule of brevity applies.

The style should be crisp and understated because, again, a flowing and discursive style is not what the reader of this genre likes, and is not really fitting in a story of high tension and rapid movement.

The emotional background in suspense stories should be

chill because such a feeling-state in the major characters is the only believable one for story people in such grim situations.

The result of these reader expectations in suspense fiction generally is a tighter, colder writing style.

Here, for example, is the total description of a new bit of setting used in a novel of mine called *The Regensburg Legacy*:

> The next morning, Friday, Dugger drove out of Stuttgart to the suburbs to the south. The sky was blue porcelain, relief after all the foul weather. A brisk breeze blew. Following small road signs with an American flag and the words KELLY BARRACKS on them, he turned off a routine German street and found himself approaching a gate to the military installation like any of a thousand others in the world. There was a high chain-link fence, a black-on-white sign, broad paving, and a guardhouse manned by smartly uniformed MPs.

There is no more description of the new setting. The plot continues immediately with Dugger's attempt to gain admittance to the installation.

While this limited amount of attention to setting, and this sort of unornamented prose, are perfectly fitting in suspense, let me ask you to pause for a moment here and give some thought to how much differently this setting segment might have been written for a romance novel. How much longer might it have been? How much looser and more flowery might the language have been? How much more emotional content—the feelings of the viewpoint character—might there have been?

I think it would have been three to five times as long, and perhaps longer. There would have been much heavier specific description of all kinds—details about the buildings and pavements, the colors of the flower boxes, the sounds of traffic, the sight of birds overhead, the smell of diesel fumes. The writing would have been looser and more ornate, and *everything* in the setting would have been related somehow to the viewpoint character's interior life, her emotional reactions to the environment.

Such differences in handling of setting are often overlooked by the unwary writer, so that even promising stories fail because their emphases and modes of delivery don't fit the genre.

HISTORICALS

Readers of historicals bring still different expectations to that genre, making different demands on the writer. In this kind of story—almost always a long, thick novel—breadth of focus, width of historical sweep, and richness of factual information are expected, even required. If you wish to write such a book, be sure to provide for:

1. Vast background content.
2. Heavy doses of minute period detail.
3. A variety of vantage points.
4. A plot deeply intertwined in the setting.

In terms of content, the setting should contain both vast historic and regional background. At the same time it is offering broad scope and panorama, it should give the reader heavy doses of setting minutiae, little tidbits about the cost of snuff in the colonies, for example, or how milady powdered her hair in those days.

Since both of these focal lengths—very long-distance and extremely close-up—are required in the historical, the writer will be forced to use both the wide-screen omniscient view "from on high" and the tightly restricted, intimate experience of the viewpoint character dealing with fine details. This will probably make the writing style itself fall somewhere between the lushness of the romance and the chill brevity of suspense.

Whatever is presented in the plot, the setting will remain very much in evidence, with the plot intertwined with it, and it will have considerable wordage devoted to it, because it is in the setting that the historic facts and ambience will be transmitted to the reader—who chooses this sort of novel largely to get such input.

The plot may be considerably tighter than in the romance,

for example, but probably will not be as rigid as in the suspense story; a strong plot will be needed to keep the long, broad-canvas story moving, but it will not be such a tightly pressing plot that characters don't have adequate time to experience (and notice) the setting details which form such an important part of the appeal for the average reader of historicals.

SCIENCE FICTION

Readers of science fiction are a bit different from those of any of the genres mentioned so far, and their expectations may give the writer more latitude than in any other genre in terms of what kind of setting and how much setting should be emphasized in the telling of the story. This is so because science fiction may have a primarily suspenseful slant or can, on occasion, be quite romantic. These varying tendencies within the broad genre can result in stories which handle setting in vastly different ways.

Virtually all science fiction, however, has the following characteristics:

1. A background of solid scientific data.
2. Extrapolation from known current facts.
3. A plot which grows out of the setting in some way.

One almost universal truth that can be seen concerning science fiction is that all the genre, from "space opera" to the weightiest technological tome, emphasizes data. In other words, in almost all science fiction the emphasis is on the factual background in the setting and the ideas tested in the plot, rather than on, say, romantic character interaction or straight physical suspense.

What does this mean to you as a potential writer of science fiction? First of all, it means you're going to have to know some cutting-edge science; you may start your research by reading a short, speculative piece in a magazine like *Omni*, but chances are that you'll soon find yourself delving into heavier publications such as *Scientific American*, which can be very heavy going indeed.

In addition, you will use your research findings to invest your setting with some technological trappings, and more often than not you will extrapolate this setting into the future from present-day science, while making sure that your plot problem grows out of the technological setting, rather than just being in the same story with it.

The point made in the last part of the preceding sentence was a whopper, so let's consider it further. What do I mean when I say the plot problem should grow out of the setting, rather than merely be in the same story with it? Simply this: It's a mistake to think that the science or technology setting for such a story is merely a backdrop; the setting should make the story go — should include the basis for the problem or quest itself.

This obviously requires that you do more than make up a glittering scientific setting and then arbitrarily stick any old story into it. The setting has to *cause* the story, almost; it has to contain the germ of the basic plot problem.

Earlier I mentioned *Ariel*, one of my novels that I liked the best when I wrote it. Although the novel sold as a "mainstream" book, it's basically science fiction put into a setting of research on artificial intelligence in computers. The story provides an example of how setting becomes the core of the plot problem, and how the two are completely tied together. The setting is a research lab in which there is a mainframe computer being modified and programmed for artificial intelligence; once this setting changes dynamically, however — and the computer asks *"Who am I?"* — the plot can never be the same again. A change in the setting has changed everything, forever.

Good science fiction almost always works like this.

Another aspect of science fiction setting, briefly alluded to previously, is the fact that the "science," wild as it might be, is rooted in real, contemporary science. That is to say, the story might turn out to be about strange clone-characters trying to take over the world; but this yarn would include in it as setting and background some information about actual chromosomal engineering and gene-changing being done in the world's labs today. The use of real, present-day research as a springboard into the extrapolated story setting is very common, and that's because the existence of some actual research now makes it easier for the reader to accept the story premise, even though it might be a wild departure from today.

STUDYING MARKETS

Often writers are encouraged to "study the markets" and "see what's selling." One of the bases for such advice lies in the genre expectations of readers such as those discussed in this chapter. It's fatal to try to handle a setting for a suspense story in the same way you would handle one for a romance, or even a science fiction story. Therefore you must know what the generalities of each genre are if you are to handle your settings in an acceptable manner.

Remember, however, that such genre expectations are somewhat general. A common mistake is to look too specifically at "what's selling," and then to slavishly copy the detail rather than the generality. For example, one might notice a colorful Caribbean setting, then write his own story against an identical colorful Caribbean setting, when what he should have done was notice the broader principle of exotic locale behind the specific Caribbean setting, then search for a *different* exotic setting that would also fit the pattern.

Most studies of genre expectations and requirements fall into this mistake of being too specific and failing to see the general principle at work. In handling setting for genre, nothing can be worse; by the time you've finished your book, the specific acceptable locale may have changed again and only the general requirement for the exotic, lushly described setting will remain.

Study the genre you want to "hit." Then search for the general rules about its setting. One flies in the face of such generalities at grave risk. But by all means also recognize the freedom of choice this study still leaves to you!

CHAPTER 6

HOW SETTING ACTS AS YOUR STORY BACKBONE

A COMMON PROBLEM IN WRITING a long story, especially something as lengthy as a novel, has to do with story *unity* or cohesion. "I have six subplots going, and how do I keep a sense of unity in my story with so many?" a writer may ask. Or: "I simply must change viewpoint several times, but what can I do to maintain a sense of coherent, cohesive story line?" Or (scariest of all!): "My story seems to be flying all to pieces, and I don't know how to hold all the diverse elements together."

Expert use of setting can often provide an answer to such questions.

Setting—especially the concrete, physical setting experienced through the senses of the characters or described in occasional panorama by the author—can provide a constant, stable, reassuringly familiar backdrop against which all manner of diverse plot developments can be played out.

In this sense, story setting functions very much like the setting of a stage play. The backdrop may be the brick walls of office buildings, with perhaps a streetlight and a mailbox as the only other features; two characters may move out in front of this setting and talk about plans to rob a bank, then exit stage left; next may come a young couple talking about his new job, and how excited they are about it. Superficially there may be no clear connection between the two bits of action that have taken place, but because they both have played against the same backdrop, the audience will be quite sure that *there is a unity here*—that the two bits of action definitely are linked in some way—

even though no overt connection has been demonstrated. The setting has done the job.

Multiplot, multiple-viewpoint novels often achieve a similar feeling of unity almost entirely by reliance on common setting as the binding factor. The suspense novels of writers like Tom Clancy and Clive Cussler rely heavily on same-setting unification. A few years before these writers attained their present popularity, Arthur Hailey made unifying setting the bedrock foundation of his novels like *Hotel* and *Airport*. In the novels of Phyllis A. Whitney, setting is always an important unifying factor as a bewildering variety of characters assail and confuse the first-person narrator; further, in the Whitney novels, the setting very often includes hidden history—past events concealed by some of the characters—whose eventual revelation is central to working out of the plot and the main character's personal problems.

Consider, for example, Cussler's breakthrough novel, *Raise The Titanic*, in which the long-sunken wrecked ship is constantly at the center of discussions, maneuvers, plans and counterattacks. If the Titanic were not at the heart of the setting as both focus and target of everyone's quest, the dozens of viewpoint changes would be hopelessly confusing.

Or consider *Hotel*, in which the very purpose of the novel is to place a wildly mixed batch of characters and plot problems within a single setting and show how the problems all work out within that unifying setting.

In the case of Whitney, try to imagine how a novel such as *The Trembling Hills* could work at all if the setting were not San Francisco at the time of the great earthquake there. Without the unification of constant references to that colorful historic setting, the multiple story lines would seem to "fly all to pieces" in apparent lack of relevance to one another.

Let me encourage you to study a number of recent novels of your own selection; look at the setting and examine the different viewpoints and plot lines. Ask yourself how many of the varying elements tie directly to one another in ways other than through reference to the setting. I think you will be surprised to see how often divergent aspects of plot and character would not be seen as related at all if they did not play against identical setting back-drops.

Further, you might want to consider how the *tone*, *mood* and *atmosphere* of setting will unify a story. From Edgar Allan Poe to Stephen King, horror writers have known this to be so. The consistent emphasis on darkness, dankness, isolation, eccentricity and occult intervention gives King's novels, for example, a unifyingly frightening feel that no single plot element or character can provide. To put this another way, in the novels of King and other horror writers, sometimes the consistent feeling of dread and fright comes not so much from what happens as it does from where it happens, and how that place feels.

Thus you can not only make your story more believable and convincing through sound use of setting, you can also unify it both in terms of making disparate plots and characters seem related and in terms of building up a story atmosphere which will cloak all characters and events within a single feeling matrix.

This is another reason why setting is so important, you see. You get not only obvious credibility advantages from proper handling of setting, but also unification of other story elements.

UNIFYING TECHNIQUES

A variety of techniques are available that will help you use your setting as a unifying "binder." We will look at six of these techniques, those used most often by writers to create a strong sense of cohesion in their stories. Study each technique, and use them to unify your own stories.

Consistent and repeated reference to a single aspect of your setting will keep that aspect uppermost in your reader's mind. Then, as you show different characters noticing this single aspect, or as you play out different scenes near it, or include a reference to it, you consistently remind the reader that, "Hey, we're in the same place, see? The same story, see?"

One example might be use of a clock tower on the main street of your story's small town. To transform the clock and its tower into a potential unifying device, you would first give it some considerable notice and description, perhaps something like this:

> Middletown's Main Street was dominated by the First National Bank's old brick clock tower, built in 1889 and a landmark to the present day. No other structure on the street stood more than two stories tall, but the clock tower extended a full three stories taller. Its dark red bricks were stained by generations of soot and rain, its conical copper roof was green from decades of corrosion. It had a clock face on all four of its sides, each face almost six feet in diameter, with ornate Roman numerals and hands festooned with spidery black curlicues. It struck every fifteen minutes and tolled out each hour, its vast and metallic voice an echo from times gone by. At night, four small spotlights shone on it, illuminating it like the rampart of a mighty old castle. Whenever anyone looked for a symbol of Middletown, they almost always came back to the clock tower, for it dominated the town; it always had, and it always would. Some said it *was* Middletown.

Such a lengthy description, as useful as it might be in building up story mood, could hardly be allowed, even in a novel, unless the tower was also being set up as a constant unifying aspect of the setting. You can be sure that the reader would "latch onto" such an elaborate description, and remember it. (Remember that lengthy descriptions ordinarily are to be avoided. When you insert one such as this for a very special reason, the reader notices immediately.)

Having thus gotten the reader's attention, you could use the clock tower again and again as a unifying reminder:

- Characters could agree to "meet under the old clock."
- Someone could hear the old clock striking the hour.
- The author could comment that the tower looked especially dark today against the rainy sky.
- Traffic might be described at some point as being backed up from First Street all the way down to the clock tower corner.

- An elderly character might comment that he feels "as old as that clock downtown on the bank corner."

I leave it to you to imagine many other ways the clock and its tower could be mentioned repeatedly in a story as a unifying factor.

Repeated reference to certain aspects of the setting by one or more characters is closely related to the technique just discussed, but a bit different. In this case, the author does not focus on a single item in the story environment such as the clock tower, but on some angle about the setting which is dominant. This might be how isolated a setting is, for example, or how grungy, or how it might be sandwiched in between a steep hillside and a fast-moving river. In such a situation, the author (through her direct description) and the characters (through taking notice in viewpoint, or in making dialogue comments) repeatedly refer to the general angle that is set up early in the story as particularly noteworthy.

Here's an example of how a general setting angle might be set up at the outset (here focusing on a town's isolation):

> Middletown stood on the prairie halfway between Junction City to the north and Emersonville to the south, eighty miles to Junction City, ninety to Emersonville. To the east and west, the next hint of "civilization" was much farther away. On a clear summer day, someone once said, you could look in any direction, for as long as you could bear it, and never see anything at all but sagebrush, rolling sand dunes, and an occasional dust devil.

Having once set up this aspect of the setting in the reader's consciousness, the author might salt into the story dozens of references like the following:

- The brilliant sunlight made her shrink from the vast distances.
- "You can't get anywhere from here in less than two hours," he said.

- She drove to the edge of town and looked out toward— nothing.
- Sleep would not come. She felt like she had been dropped into the middle of the Sahara desert. . . .
- An old pickup truck, coated with the red dust of a million desolate miles, rolled in from the empty prairie to the north.
- The town felt like a place on a distant planet, so isolated was it.

Again, you may come up with small references that would do a better job than any of these in referring back to isolation as a general, unifying aspect of the setting.

Continual, subtle expansion on a detail or aspect of the setting will also serve to keep it in focus as a unifying element. How would such a process work? Rather than beginning with a large description, as in the case of the clock tower mentioned above, you would start small, and build. As the story went along, the element of the setting chosen for such treatment would grow larger and larger in the reader's awareness.

As an example, in one of my earlier novels titled *Katie, Kelly and Heck*, I had five distinct plot lines and some dozen viewpoints working from quite early in the book. Although all the events took place in the same small town—one unifying factor—I worried that something further was needed to assure an additional sense of unity. The setting device I discovered, and built more importantly as the story progressed, was a back-alley whisky still which no single character considered centrally important.

I first showed the still, freshly loaded and beginning to cook a new batch of sour-mash whisky. It was simply mentioned as being located in the alley.

A chapter later, I showed a secondary character examining the still in more detail. This time I revealed the ownership of the apparatus and its importance to him. Two more sentences of description were added to what had been provided in the earlier segment, this time telling the capacity of the still, its temperature, and its internal pressure. I also described a pressure gauge on the equipment.

Fifteen pages later, I showed the still being sabotaged—the pressure valves being closed, the heat starting to increase, and the aforementioned pressure gauge beginning to rise.

From that point, with metronomic regularity, I returned in brief segments to the still, unattended in the alley; each time, a bit more description was added, and each time it was noted that the temperature was still higher, the internal pressure continuing to rise toward the red line on the gauge. While all the characters in the story went about their own business, and the physical setting changed from place to place around the town, the repeating, expanding progress reports on the still, described objectively from a viewpoint "on high," maintained a central setting detail focus point for the book until very late in the story when—you guessed it—the still exploded, bringing everyone's attention back to it.

In your story the central aspect of setting might be a house, a room in that house, a street, a gathering storm. Whatever it might be, if you first merely mention it but then continually return to it with greater and greater attention to descriptive detail, you may be sure your reader will focus on it and cling to it as a unifying factor in your yarn.

Ongoing references to different aspects of the setting which have something in common is slightly different again. Here, rather than seeking different ways to refer to generally the same phenomenon, as in our examples above about isolation, you provide the reader with different looks at various parts of the setting, building a complete and detailed picture, finally, by a process of accretion.

For example, you might show a factory worker in a small town paying his home rent to an office operated by the same company that pays his wages. A bit later, you might show the same worker shopping and getting additional credit at the company store. Still later, you might have him taking his sick child to the clinic (the only one in town) operated by the company. And later yet you might describe how the local newspaper is run by an editor who happens to be the brother-in-law of the owner of the local company. As you added references to other aspects of the setting, a composite picture would emerge which would give the reader a convincing picture of a "company town" where anyone trying to be independent would face grave odds indeed.

Such a technique is very convincing to readers, incidentally, because it allows them to experience and draw conclusions about a story setting in the same way they operate with real-world environments: by collecting small bits of data and finally drawing conclusions from them. In addition, of course, the quiet drumbeat-like presentation of different aspects, all pointing to the same generality about the setting, give the story a wonderful cohesiveness.

Careful comparison-reference back to what the setting was before it changed can allow setting to remain a unifying factor even when the actual setting changes. Suppose, for example, a basis of your plot lies partly in the stress caused to the characters because they are forced to move from the city to an unfamiliar rural area (change in setting causing the plot). In such a circumstance, you would be required to describe the city setting in order later to show how different it is from the new rural one. All well and good, but the sudden change from urban to rural in the middle of the story might create a sharp feeling of discontinuity—loss of unity—for your reader.

In such a situation, the unity of the plot problem would be emphasized by your references to the conflicted feelings in the characters as caused by the move; by comparing new setting versus the old in an author-objective passage or two; by having characters talk about the new setting and how it differs from the previous one; or by having characters homesick for the old setting, talking about how good it was, how unfamiliar they are with the new. In this way, the change in setting would itself become a constant setting reference point!

In my novel *Katie, Kelly and Heck*, mentioned earlier, Katie Blanscombe is dislocated from Cleveland, Ohio, to a sorry, isolated little outpost in Arizona, where she gets into all kinds of trouble because she simply does not understand the new territory. In the course of the novel, I found it useful to have Katie fall prey to homesickness again and again, and to criticize her new hometown as being barbaric when compared with Cleveland. Thus, even as Katie moved from a boardinghouse to a hotel, and from poverty to ownership of a restaurant, and from nervous self-restraint to a scene in which she danced and kicked up her heels on a cafe stage, her basic personality was kept unified and consistent—and her essential personal problem kept in focus—by the fact that she kept being homesick and kept moaning about "this dreadful little town," comparing the setting to the one she had left in Cleveland.

You may think of other examples in which the very emphasis on change in setting becomes a unifying factor of its own. The story of a wagon train going west, for example, might pass through a number of contrasting macrosettings—grasslands, prairie, deserts, rivers, mountains—and might in part be held together because the microsetting, the wagon train itself, remained much the same. Additional unity might be given such a story also, by having the characters notice and comment on the changing backdrop during the journey, saying things like, "I thought the rainy weather on the prairie was bad until we reached this Godforsaken desert, where it never seems to get below a hundred degrees."

Showing that the setting is contributing to the course of events can add unity to a story. Here the trick often is to have characters in the story point this out, saying things like the following:

- "This couldn't happen except in Middletown."
- "A company town always enforces its rules on trouble-makers."
- "If that wall of snow and ice starts to move, we're trapped."
- "A mother-lode discovery like this one always brings in the lawless element, and we should have expected it."
- "When the store was robbed last Tuesday, it changed our lives forever."

There are occasions when it may seem like overkill to have characters comment on the impact of setting on plot—when it's so obvious that mention of it may sound silly. But real people tend to belabor the obvious when they're under stress, and realistic story people will, too. So as you build credibility sometimes by allowing characters to worry aloud about obvious problems, you may also improve the sense of story unity by pointing out to the reader that the setting is holding things together by contributing to story happenings.

A SETTING EMPHASIS TO AVOID

If you believe from this discussion that I consider setting a primary unifying factor in many novels, you are absolutely correct. As long as each mention of setting is done briefly—ordinarily a few lines at a time, at most—I believe constant reference to setting will have multiple salutary effects on your copy.

However, there are times in your story when you must be careful *not* to dwell on setting, especially avoiding mention of any new aspects of it. This is when you are just opening a new story segment which involves transition in viewpoint or immediate locale.

Suppose, for example, that you are writing a novel in multiple viewpoint, with multiple plot lines and numerous settings. Suppose further that you have been away from character Martha's viewpoint and plot for a number of pages, and now wish to return to her.

Making such a transition in story focus and interest is difficult for your reader. It is incumbent upon you to make the change as painless and unconfusing as possible. The last thing you want to do is confuse him. If you open up your new segment returning to Martha's viewpoint and emphasizing the new setting she is in, the new and unfamiliar detail makes the reader's reorientation more difficult and potentially confusing.

To put this another way, you're asking the reader to make a hard enough jump in going from, say, character Sam's viewpoint and locale back to Martha's. You want to make it as easy as possible. How would you do this?

1. Avoid introducing new setting detail at the outset. This

in itself will eliminate one possibly disorienting element in your transition.

2. Remind the reader how your character was feeling when last seen. Given any clue at all, your reader will recall how your viewpoint character was feeling when the story was last in her viewpoint. By mentioning this same feeling again when you return to her viewpoint, you give the reader a vital "connection point" for a successful transition.

3. Refer to a unifying aspect of setting already established. This will give the reader a familiar landmark as a point of reorientation. Only well after you have eased the reader into the changed viewpoint — and reminded him of the setting in terms already familiar to him — can you risk the potentially disorienting tactic of adding new details about the setting.

Let's look at an example to clarify number three. Suppose you were returning to Martha's viewpoint downtown after you had devoted a few chapters to other viewpoints elsewhere, perhaps on the far outskirts of your town. You might ease the initial transition something like this (italics added for emphasis):

> *Still angry and worried* as a result of her argument with Bill, Martha parked her car on Main Street a block from the center of town. As she got out of the car, *the familiar sound of the old clock on the bank corner* reached her ears. It was tolling noon. *Fighting tears of frustration*, she walked toward the *tall, sooty brick tower where the clock had tolled for a century.* . . .

The first italicized words avoid any new detail and reestablish Martha's point of view by harking back to the last time she was seen in the story, reminding the reader of the exact same emotion Martha was experiencing then. This returns the reader to Martha's viewpoint in the least difficult way possible. (This matter of identifying a character's feelings — her *emotional focus* — is a subject we will consider in greater detail in chapter eleven.)

The second group of italicized words further eases the transition by mentioning something in the physical environment that is already familiar to the reader from earlier parts of the story: the clock.

The third and fourth brief segments elaborate briefly on the first two.

This works. But imagine how confused the reader might be at such a time of transition if the author had begun the new segment by describing previously unmentioned aspects of the setting, such as, say, false storefronts along Main Street, advertising signs, small shrubs dying from a drouth, or a beggar often seen on the curb. Introduction of such new setting detail would only disorient the reader. When making a transition, the familiar must be emphasized first!

Later in your story section, of course, you might well add a few new details about the setting, but only after you had written a reorientation paragraph (or two) would it be safe to do so.

But how would such tactics work if Martha had really traveled far from her small town while we were away from her viewpoint for a chapter or two? What if she had gone all the way to London, for example?

The same basic procedure would work. Here's how that kind of transitional opening might be worded:

> *Still angry and worried* a full week after her argument with Bill, Martha felt very much alone as she walked along the Thames. She looked across the river toward Big Ben in its ancient tower that so symbolized London. The great old clock began to toll the hour. It sounded so *familiar, so much like the old clock on the bank corner back home,* that her eyes filled with tears. . . .

Later, of course, new details about the London setting would be added a few at a time, as necessary. But reader reorientation takes precedence over any such additional detail.

SUGGESTED EXERCISE

An exercise might help you firm up your understanding of the techniques outlined in this chapter. While no single bit of homework is guaranteed to touch all the bases, the following exercise

is one that has helped a great many writing students. Perhaps
you would like to try it:

1. Carefully write an author-objective description of a major, noteworthy aspect of a setting, something like the clock
tower used in illustrations in this chapter. Make this description,
up to three hundred words, as vivid and detailed as you can,
appealing to as many of the reader's senses as possible, and try
to tie the physical description to some feeling or mood you want
to set up in a story.
2. Add two or three brief, cogent paragraphs to this description from the viewpoint of a character, adding a bit about how
the setting looks to the character, or how it makes her feel, or
what it makes her think about. (Not more than a hundred additional words for this.)
3. Simply list five additional and related aspects of setting
you might use in the same story if you were pursuing it through
several additional chapters.
4. Imagine that you have been away from your chosen viewpoint character's head and heart for twenty-five pages, and now
wish to return to her, in viewpoint, near the place where your
major, noteworthy aspect of setting is located. Write the first
four sentences of a segment that would return the reader to this
viewpoint and locale.

Having done these things, put the pages aside temporarily and
reread this chapter on setting. Then go back to each of your
assignment pages with a critical eye and ask yourself these questions:

1. Is the noteworthy aspect of setting which I selected a
good and central one for the story I want to tell? Is it interesting?
Unusual? Sure to stand out?
2. Have I described it vividly, in as few pointed words as
possible?
3. Is my list of additional features (to be added later) the
best I can come up with? Taken altogether, do they tend to
complete a coherent, evocative picture of this place and/or time?
4. In my "returning episode," have I carefully noted my
imagined character's emotion? Have I carefully mentioned only

that part of the setting which forms my central, noteworthy aspect?

If your answer to any of these questions is "no," then rewrite! It's important to have the material in this chapter clearly in your mind before moving on to other dynamic ways you can use setting to improve your story.

CHAPTER 7

HOW TO USE
SETTING TO
ADVANCE PLOT

It's far too easy to fall into the trap of thinking of setting as a fixed and static aspect of your story. As implied in some of our earlier discussion, setting is not necessarily static at all: The weather may change, a storm may develop or collapse or move on; the background attitudes of characters may be radically altered by plot events; virtually anything may happen to alter the environment in which the story is playing out. Just as a story's plot must move forward and its characters must experience things, and change, so too the setting can seldom be allowed to stand in the background as a totally predictable, immutable element. When writers get bogged down in a story, sometimes it's because they have forgotten all this.

ADVANCEMENT OF PLOT

Setting can be used in several ways to help you advance your plot.

First, you can emphasize setting in a new way, bringing out a previously unseen problem. Imagine that you have built a story setting involving a small business depicted as thrifty, energetic and competitive against larger firms. Now think about how you might complicate and advance the plot by putting much greater emphasis on the company's competitive situation and the size of its rival firms. Suddenly your reader (and perhaps some of your characters) might begin seeing the company setting as precarious rather than comfortable, as too small to compete successfully rather than as a cozy Ma-and-Pa operation, as a place to escape from rather than a place to settle in. Once you have begun emphasizing these ways of looking at your setting, imagine how your plot might be advanced in terms of character problem (and reader interest).

It might come in a passage like this:

> The constant jangling of telephones suddenly struck Calvin as discordant, harshly demanding. He saw the driven expressions on some of his coworkers' faces, understanding for the first time how desperately all of them were working to stay ahead of the Acme Company down the street. He smelled frightened sweat—his own—and felt his stomach tighten as Meg hurried in from the front office, carrying a stack of change-orders. He had seen change-orders a thousand times, but suddenly they looked different to him. Now, instead of a challenge, they represented a threat. What if that stack of papers represented cancellations that could sink the Blodgett Company ... and threaten his future?

Now the office setting is no longer comfortable. Now today's business is not merely important, but a matter of life and death. Now the meeting this afternoon must perhaps deal with a crucial marketing decision, rather than with routine business. By emphasizing the setting in a new way, you may dictate inescapable results in the immediate plot. To put this another way, by emphasizing the setting in a new way, you make something happen in your plot.

Or as another example, suppose you're writing a story about a small mining town in the Old West, bound inside a tight river canyon by high mountains on both east and west. You might first describe this town setting as secure, walled in from intruders, protected from the winter weather and cool and shady in the summer. But you could easily use the same setting to advance your plot simply by choosing to emphasize other aspects of it: The great gray massiveness of the surrounding mountains, their enormous bulk seeming to hang poised over the town, ready to wipe it out with a landslide at any moment; the way the tight river canyon walls in the town and makes it impossible for anyone inside the town to see approaching attackers; how the encapsulation of the town in its stone cocoon has made its people closed-minded and suspicious.

Even more dramatic in terms of advancing the plot is the introduction of new aspects of the setting not previously seen, so that your reader worries more and your major characters are forced to take some unexpected action.

Suppose again that your setting is the mountain town described above, with only its friendlier aspects identified. Suppose that Ted, your viewpoint character, learns something previously unknown about the setting, as in the following example:

> "I love the mountain behind the town," Ted told Maxwell. "It gives a feeling of solidity—strength. You just know this town is as solid as that granite."
>
> Maxwell's face twisted with pain. "Solid as that granite, eh? That's all *you* know, my friend."
>
> "What do you mean?" Ted shot back.
>
> Maxwell squinted upward at the rock face overhanging the buildings, and pointed. "You've seen those deep fissures, the shadowy cracks in the face?"
>
> "Of course. What . . ."
>
> "Those cracks go deep, Ted. It isn't generally known, but the entire face of that mountain is crumbling. That granite is rotten. Give us the slightest earth tremor, or even a heavy and prolonged rainstorm, and the face of that seemingly solid mountain could fall right onto this town—wipe it out in an instant."

This new aspect of the setting changes everything. It has to jolt your character into a reassessment of everything, and possibly change the course of the story from that moment forward.

Often most dramatic of all is the basic, abrupt change in the setting itself. Such a change upsets all expectations and must result in new plot developments.

When I mention change in the setting, I am not talking about actually moving the locale of the story, although you might elect to do that sometimes, too. Here I refer to having something change drastically in the essential makeup of the existing story backdrop. For example, rather than having Jennifer move from Peoria to San Francisco, we would stay in Peoria, but have three closely timed murders create an atmosphere of terror and suspicion inside the same general physical environment. Or, rather than leaving our car race at the Indianapolis 500 and changing the setting to Dayton, Ohio, we would stay at Indianapolis but show the sky clouding over, threatening a dangerous downpour on the track.

Or perhaps the setting could change in a way similar to the following example:

> The Sparger family had been near the heart of power in Middletown for more than fifty years. Ted's father and his father before him had been leaders of the local Democratic Party's machinery, and had always had a voice in political decisions. It was this political power that had made Jim so confident he could get the block of Main Street rezoned to allow him to tear down the old bank building and sell the property for a new apartment complex.
>
> By midnight, however, as the election returns kept coming in, he saw that everything in this comfortable world of his had suddenly changed.
>
> "We've lost," the Democratic chairman told him bitterly around 1 A.M. "This is no longer our town. We have no control now. Nothing is ever going to be the same again."

Thus the physical setting is the same, but the cultural-political setting has become vastly different, and for people like Jim it is really no longer the same setting at all.

Changes inside the setting are almost always threatening to story characters in some way, and because they are threatened, those characters do something about it. And when characters do something about it, your plot is jostled off dead center.

A change in the setting can also be used much more dramatically, of course, to make the plot action change as well, and instantly. If your quiet suburban hospital suddenly catches fire, this change in the setting has instantaneous results in the plot as people run for safety and/or try to put the fire out.

What's the moral here? Simply this: Any time you feel a need to move your plot along, look at the possibility of introducing a real or just perceived change in the setting you've been using, or changing the way you've been describing the setting. A dark cloud scuds across the sun, plunging the street into darkness; a character learns that someone died in this rented house last year; suddenly the town no longer feels friendly; a rock tumbles and a landslide begins to gain momentum. In each case a different reader perception of the setting has started us toward movement in the plot.

ENHANCEMENT OF TENSION

In virtually all such situations the change does more than motivate characters to do something, thus advancing the plot; it also increases dramatic tension in both the characters and your reader. You can capitalize on this fact by consciously tailoring your setting change to increase tension in any of the following ways (or with a combination of them):

1. by darkening the mood of the story
2. by introducing new threatening element(s)
3. by creating mystery
4. by overturning previous character expectations
5. by demanding immediate action.

In an earlier chapter, a suspense novel by John Miles, *The Night Hunters*, was mentioned in an illustration. The same novel might be used as a source of illustrations of all the points just listed.

Two paragraphs in chapter two of the novel begin to darken the mood as follows:

> She wished . . . that she hadn't found that Bartelson had died by his own hand. There was something still depressing about the picture that the scant facts portrayed: a man coming west, as they said, to make good, and doing

all the "right" things—serving in the army, opening his own business, serving the community. But for Bartelson it had all gone sour. Ruth tried to imagine how it must have been, staking one's life in this remote place, walking every day under these brooding old trees, feeling the heat of late summer suck the energy out of every pore, watching the forces that no one could understand take everything that had been worked for, saved, built against the future.

She shivered again, for no reason, and hugged her arms about herself. . . .

The first paragraph breaks almost perfectly in half, first recapping new and worrisome information just learned about the setting; then, with the "Ruth tried to imagine" sentence, moving into the viewpoint character's feelings and using emotionally charged words like "remote" and "brooding" to darken the mood.

Such work on the mood of the setting is especially important in a novel such as *The Night Hunters*, set in a small southeastern Oklahoma town which ordinarily would not be thought of as threatening. Many short passages clearly designed to darken the mood are found throughout the novel.

The book is, however, not merely a mood piece but a suspense novel. Only a few pages after the segment quoted above, another character close to Ruth is seen driving home late at night. Here there is another touch of the darkness of the first paragraph, and then the introduction of a new threatening element:

Preoccupied with her and his own feelings, Doug drove the few blocks to the little house he had rented. He did not think deeply into the questions she had raised about the missing records or seeming lies, because he well enough understood the clannish, suspicious nature of the people of Noble. It was simply one more manifestation of their kind of hate, he told himself. It meant nothing more. . . .

Because of his preoccupation, Doug Bennett did not see the black Ford cruise quietly down the street moments after he had gone inside. The car was parked and the engine shut off. The lone occupant remained behind the wheel, watching. Long after the lights had gone out in Doug's house, the shadowy figure remained in the car, watching, moving now and then as a pint bottle was raised, sipped from and put back on the seat.

Such a passage, of course, creates mystery, too.

Setting or a change in setting can also be used, as previously stated, to *overturn character expectations*. Later in the same novel, the character Ruth Baxter expected to leave the town of Noble on a short trip. But her plan was thwarted just at the end of a previous chapter. Now, having been out of her viewpoint and setting for about a dozen pages, the reader is returned to her at the start of chapter nine like this:

> The impulse was to scream — to scream and keep on screaming, to let the fear burst out. Ruth fought it and held it back by the tiniest margin of control.
>
> The tunnel was less than ten feet in diameter. The only illumination was an urnlike, battery-operated fishing lantern on the loose gravel-and-earth floor. Its yellowish light shone against chalky stone walls, seeping water here and there, braced in X patterns with heavy, rough-cut timbers gone black from age and rot. . . .
>
> Ruth, her hands tied in front of her, was made prisoner to one of the huge support beams by another length of rope looped through her arms and tied to the beam. . . .

Here the transition is eased for the reader exclusively through identification of a carry-over emotion from when Ruth was last seen. But the setting is new and totally unfamiliar, a tactical fiction situation we earlier warned against because it creates confusion. But here the gambit is acceptable and even desirable because clearly one of the author's goals is to make the reader experience just a little of the fright and disorientation that Ruth herself is feeling. In effect, the near-vertigo experienced by the reader in being plunged headlong into a new and alien setting works here, because confusion is exactly a part of the effect being sought. In such a drastic change, the character Ruth obviously is not—and will never be—the same; all her expectations and assumptions have been altered forever by finding herself suddenly in this new setting.

Finally, and perhaps the easiest method of all to understand, you can increase story tension with a change in your setting that *demands immediate action*. Such action-demanding setting changes are often dynamic and highly dramatic, like the following:

- Setting: a quiet town. But then the dam breaks above it.
- Setting: a small hospital. But then a deadly epidemic breaks out.
- Setting: a peaceful street. But then gunshots are heard.
- Setting: a nice old house. But then the eviction notice is served.

I leave it to you to conjure up any number of other static settings in which a change dramatically increases tension.

THE POWER OF REPETITION

Although the emphasis in this chapter has been primarily on dynamic setting—setting in change or with changing perception—it is also possible to increase story tension simply by drumming away at a static setting that is threatening or scary to begin with, such as in the novels of Stephen King. Often there is no really new development in the setting at the times when the story intensifies. What we get instead is further moody description of the same setting, which has a cumulative emotional effect. To reduce the process to absurdity: One cobweb across the face means nothing, but a dozen may mean a haunted house; one momentarily glimpsed light in the old mansion may be a trick of moonlight, but several such sightings almost surely mean something dire is afoot.

By all means, then, you should realize that handling of setting can be an invaluable tool for you in increasing plot tension and making things happen. It's axiomatic in fiction that characters make things happen in the plot. But it's equally true that setting can motivate characters. So you needn't always look inside your character's mind for motive; sometimes it might be simpler to examine your story environment, and do something with it that *forces* mood to darken, action to take place, or character to get moving.

All of which brings us to a closer look at the way setting forms and motivates character. That's the business of chapter eight.

CHAPTER 8

HOW SETTING
AFFECTS CHARACTER

IT MAY SEEM A BIT STRANGE to you that a separate chapter should be devoted to setting and its impact on character when it's been clear from the outset of this book that setting obviously has such impact. We have already seen how setting affects story characters in a variety of ways, potentially playing a part in their background, expectations, beliefs, hopes, ideals, problems and goals. Here, however, we want to take a deeper and more precise look at setting's impact on your story people and to point out how you should work to make setting and character harmonious.

The use of certain settings often tends to foreordain certain kinds of characters. This is because of reader expectations of the type discussed back in chapter five.

While there are exceptions to every rule, one of the most obvious examples of setting predicting a certain kind of character is the traditional western. Today you may find more short, scruffy and even "antiheroic" male leads in the traditional western setting, but the vast majority of male leads in the latest western novels are still close to the stereotype introduced all the way back in Owen Wister's *The Virginian*, the man who told someone to "smile when you say that." This character, predicted by the setting, is close to Gary Cooper in *High Noon*, or Alan Ladd in *Shane*. He is a loner, brave, soft-spoken, slow to anger, self-reliant and incredibly competent in outdoor skills and gunmanship; he is Anglo-Saxon, tall, blond or sandy-haired more often than not, vaguely in his 30s, with a background that has alienated and slightly embittered him, and possibly put him on the wrong side of an unjust legal system. Usually he has no permanent home, and owns little more than his horse and what he can pack into his saddlebags, if that much. He is a fundmamentally decent man who respects women and the underdog. He seldom seeks a fight but backs down for no man.

This prototype of the western hero does not endure simply because it seems to work in terms of reader expectation. It also works because such a character is completely in harmony with the traditional western setting; the mythic "Old West" is the kind of setting that would produce such a man, and such a man is the kind who would best survive in the Old West environment. His ideals—individualism, truthfulness, self-reliance—are the values that fueled the American psyche during the country's great expansion into its western frontier. In short, the traditional western hero is true to his setting.

Thus the setting can be a predictor of character. Publishers of romance fiction, for example, see this clearly. Some romance editors issue detailed "tip sheets" which define not only the kind of setting they want for their stories, but details about desired lead characters. Setting and character have been carefully outlined to "fit" one another.

One such publishing house recently said it wanted its stories to feature an urban or suburban woman, single, age twenty-eight or so, with a dismaying and unhappy love affair or marriage in her background; she is allowed a lively sexual appetite, but shouldn't act upon it except with the man she learns to love in the course of the story. Another publishing house said it wants younger women in college or blue-collar work situations, and expects such heroines to have more vivid sexual exploits. Still another line features older women in highly professional occupational settings, and for such characters problems in their professional lives must somehow dovetail with romantic entanglements—which, given their experiences, they should approach more cautiously than their younger sisters in the genre. And so it goes. The existence of such tip sheets proving that editors realize the intimate relationship between setting and character.

SETTING PREDESTINES CHARACTER

The impact of setting on character goes well beyond tip sheets and genre expectations, however, and you as a writer of fiction should remember that. Setting — in real life as well as in fiction — tends to form character in ways you can analyze and use in your work.

This was brought home to me most forcefully a number of years ago when, as a journalist, I was given the assignment of doing a twenty-county tour of Oklahoma to ask questions of the person on the street for a series of newspaper stories on "the mood of the state."

This was no small task, and I approached it with some trepidation. The reason was not simply the size of the task, but the fact that Oklahoma is a border state, quite different in its farm belt north and tourist campground south, its wooded hill country in the east and dusty open plains in the west. I sensed — but did not fully appreciate at first — the fact that a state with such drastic differences in topography, incomes and occupations might offer a bewildering variety of outlooks and opinions.

I set out to the western sections first, driving across vast, dusty, open prairie where you can see another car on the road five miles ahead, and a distant farm silo may be the only relief from a barren horizon. On my first day I visited three small rural towns, parking near the drugstore or courthouse and buttonholing passersby, ready with my notebook and list of questions.

To my surprise and delight, almost every one of these "plains people" responded with a cautious but open attitude; they were almost uniformly friendly and willing to help by expressing opinions. They seemed generally to trust me at once, and take me at face value.

This assignment was not going to be as hard as I had feared, I thought as I worked through other parts of the prairie country.

About three days later, I worked through the southern part of the state, visiting tourist campgrounds, fishing cabins, and little towns catering to sportsmen and sightseers. Again I found that the people were friendly. But then I drove farther east into the hill country.

I love the hills and mountains, and I grieve to report it, but the deeper I moved into tightly hill-bound terrain, visiting small hamlets dense with trees flourishing in the dark shade of overhanging cliffs and bluffs, the more chilly my reception became. Gone was the open, trusting attitude of the plains, and instead I met narrowed eyes of suspicion, sharply hostile counterquestions, and a growing number of outright refusals to so much as "talk about talking." There were open, friendly people, to be sure, but suddenly they were in a distinct minority. There were times when I felt like I had been plunged into a scene from the movie *Deliverance*.

Later I moved out of the hill country and into the northern farm belt, where attitudes toward a stranger like me seemed halfway between those I had met earlier. Only then did something begin to dawn on me with greater impact than ever before. Roughly, the realization (and I hesitate to admit I had been so dumb as not to have known it long before) went like this: "Hill people and plains people are *different*."

Why? Psychologists and social historians probably have a much better answer than I do. Surely it can't be as simple as the fact that life on the plains is marked by open horizons, vast winds, and a sky that comes down to eye level, while life in the hills is closed-in, almost hermetic at times, more isolated from the broad view.

Whatever. The basic fact is what's useful to us as writers, and that is simple enough: *Define the kind of setting a character is to be found in, and by so doing you go far toward defining the kind of character it must be.*

It may be such an obvious fact that we sometimes forget it. In more than two decades of teaching fiction, I shudder to think of the number of times I have encountered story characters like the backwoods girl who had never been out of her valley, but spoke in a brisk, "Britishy" accent; or the college-president character who dressed and acted like a gross and illiterate idiot, or the working cowboy set in an eastern courtroom and brilliantly defending a suspect in a complex lawsuit. We forget the strong link between setting and character formation only at grave peril; readers usually are quick to balk at believing story people who appear completely out of tune with their setting.

Does this mean that you should attempt to delineate characters who are perfectly typical of their story setting? By no means. If you try to do so, you risk creating stereotypes rather than vital story people, creating only dull and predictable characters. What you must aim for is the credible, not the stereotypical.

PROTOTYPES AND STEREOTYPES

Ordinarily this means that you should be aware of reader expectations in the traditional genres, and also the kind of people most typical of various real settings. It will help you in making characters and settings harmonious if you do some real-life observing and then draw up a "setting list" for your desired character.

Suppose, for example, you wish to create a character who is a famed brain surgeon. You might immediately draw a character who is a tall, middle-aged man, with gray hair, a distinguished manner, a big country home, and a workplace environment in a huge city hospital. This is all believable enough. It might work. But it is also predictable — and a bit dull.

So let's suppose for a moment that you haven't been paying attention to this chapter, and try to create a more memorable character-and-setting combination without real-world study or the knowledge that character and setting must in some way fit one another. Your new character, in such circumstances, might turn out to be a short, fat, unkempt teenager with a bad case of the shakes who spends most of his time in the pool hall, lives under a railroad bridge, and practices medicine in a clinic serving a rural community of 300 souls.

Of course I grossly exaggerate for the sake of illustration. But stranger setting-character combinations have been known in student manuscripts.

How would you avoid both the character who is credible

but dully predictable and the character who is unbelievable both in terms of his fit to the environment and the credibility of his story setting?

First you would make real-life observations. I suspect you would find things like the following about famed brain surgeons:

- They tend to be mature men. *But there are women in the field.*
- They almost always work in major hospitals in very large urban centers. *But some work in large clinics that happen to be located in smaller communities.*
- They work killingly long hours.
- They are extremely well paid—most are wealthy.
- They tend to live in large suburban homes. *But some live on ranches and some in inner-city apartments.*
- They deal daily with life-and-death situations.
- Most are in private, individual practice. *But some are members of medical firms or clinic teams.*
- Most are dedicated, and love—and live—their work. *But a few are at the burnout stage, longing to escape the pressurized life.*
- They come from well-educated family backgrounds. *But a few represent the first person from their family ever to go beyond high school.*
- They drive Mercedes and Lincoln cars. *But some drive pickup trucks, and some don't own a car at all.*

Having begun to create such a "prototype list" from actual observation, rather than from what you think you already know, you would have the stuff to begin drawing a character in a credible but not stereotypical environment. You might be able to begin creating a character who is a woman, five feet tall, the first of her family ever to attain a college education, who drives her Ford Bronco to the big clinic on the edge of a small rural community every morning. She might live on a ranch, and she might be suffering from premature professional burnout after several years of working seventeen-hour days in the operating room.

Now, having done this, I would suggest that you take further steps. You should make personal contact with a brain surgeon — or some other surgeon with a highly specialized craft — and try to spend some time with him (or her) in order to see and better understand his typical setting. Ideally you would see his home, meet his family if any, ride to work with him one day, ask questions about his background and beliefs, and even seek permission to stand beside the scrub nurse in the surgical arena and witness the environment in which he works. (I did this — with great hesitancy — for a medical novel once, and it was not as scary as I had imagined it would be; I didn't even faint.)

With all this research behind you, I suspect you would create a brain surgeon character who was not only more vivid than you might otherwise have been able to make her, but you would also have a story setting rich in the kind of detail that convinces the reader and enhances the character.

Even if you are not quite willing to go this far in making sure the wedding of setting and character is a good one, go as far as you can! Don't let laziness or shyness hold you back. In the extreme, remember that the New York City corporate executive is *ipso facto* not the same as the college English teacher at a rural Kansas junior college; and remember further that ordinarily you couldn't just switch the two characters, moving the executive to Kansas and the teacher to New York. Look long and hard at your setting, and grow characters out of it. Or look long and hard at your character and provide him with a setting that fits. Just don't ignore their relationship; to do so is to risk having unbelievable characters in a good setting, or good characters in an unbelievable setting.

CASTING AGAINST SETTING

"But" — you may be protesting — "what about that western character I just read about who was a little weasel from Chicago? Or that brain surgeon — for the luvva Mike! — whose story setting was a ranch in Arizona? Or how, Bickham, do you explain the success of the character Dr. Joel Fleischman in the popular TV show *Northern Exposure*, a young Jewish doctor in the godforsaken setting of Cicely, Alaska? Where is the harmony of setting and character in any of these examples?"

Such notable exceptions don't change the rule. They only prove that no rule is absolute, and that sometimes, with good reason, a writer can take a big risk. Such examples as cited above illustrate the process of *casting against setting* for the sake of surprise and contrast. The technique has notable triumphs, and you may wish to try it. You should be warned, however, that you walk the precipice of incredibility every time you do, and there are many failed experiments of this type for every one that works.

Parenthetically, I don't know about the weasel western character or the brain surgeon on a ranch. But Dr. Joel, in *Northern Exposure*, gets his humor and sympathy not just from being out of harmony with outback Alaska, but because he is so perfectly a product of his fictional New York City background setting. To put this another way, Joel doesn't fit his present setting, but that's a large part of the point—his continuing plot problem. On the other side of the same dramatic card, his character would not work in this predicament if he did not act *exactly* as his stated background setting ("I'm a New York City Jewish boy.") suggests. Joel fits his background, the setting from which he has been transplanted, very well indeed, and that's why he is effective as a character out of his element.

You can probably think of many other successful fiction characters who seemed to be cast against their setting. Sometimes they were; other times they are shown out of harmony only with a particular setting and were perfectly consistent when considered against the larger setting of their entire life. Wherever the truth lies, however, casting radically against setting remains a dangerous tactic.

USING SETTING TO CHANGE A CHARACTER

Whether the setting changes during the course of a story or remains essentially the same, it can cause changes in your character's perceptions, feelings, thoughts, motivations and actions.

A moment's reflection will show why this is so. We live immersed in the physical world, dozens and perhaps hundreds of impressions entering our consciousness at every instant. Because no single mind could absorb and meaningfully process all these impressions, our conscious mind ignores many of these stimuli, and gives many others only the briefest notice before dismissing them. It is even possible to act upon some aspect of our environment without consciously giving it much thought.

As an example of ignoring stimuli flowing in from our environment or setting, consider the background music piped into many shopping malls and stores. Often, we simply don't even hear it. Or suppose you happen to live on a busy street, with constant traffic sounds; unless there is a siren or a particularly loud sound, you seldom notice the routine noise at all. Similarly, we get so accustomed to seeing some routine things in our daily lives that we seem not to notice them at all: the trees in the park, perhaps, or the familiar old elm in the front yard, or (tragically, perhaps) the habitual look of strain or pain on a loved one's face.

As to the mechanism by which we take only the briefest notice and then jettison thought about a stimulus, I refer you to the television commercial. Have you ever noticed how you sometimes forget to press the mute button on your remote control because your mind has muted the message already?

But how can someone act upon some aspect of her setting without much, if any, conscious thought? Again, your own experience can provide you with examples. Perhaps a prime one might be the way you drive your car on a familiar route. Haven't you ever had the common experience of getting home after such a jaunt and realizing that you have no recollection whatsoever of changing lanes, making turns, dodging other drivers, or even stopping for traffic lights? You noticed, and acted, without really knowing it.

It has even been suggested that post-surgical depression in some cases may be caused by the fact that the unconscious mind remains alert during anesthesia, that it remembers quite vividly the pain of the operation, and takes time to get over that trauma.

If our real-life setting can din into us in all these ways, then isn't it clear that we are never really out of the impact zone of our environment? And isn't it even more obvious that our setting can affect our personality and actions at those times when we are not conscious of it?

The lesson to be learned, then, is that you as a writer of fiction can tailor changes in your story setting to affect your character. You not only can do so, but almost must do so, if your story is to function like real life. So let's look at the most obvious ways you can consciously craft your setting in order to change a character.

Moving your character into a different setting is the most obvious and perhaps simplest device for using setting as an agent of character change. To be sure, thrusting a character into a new and different setting does not guarantee he will change; in adventure fiction, where the action is the thing, a character can be pushed into all kinds of wild setting variations and yet be the same person throughout. (Think of Indiana Jones.) But if you are writing another kind of fiction where character change is desired, you can show the character first noticing the change in setting, then definitely reacting as a result of taking notice.

This means that you must not only delineate the new setting and how it differs from the previous one, but you should show the character taking note of the change. Ordinarily, if you are in the character's viewpoint, this will be no problem. Just make sure that you include clauses like "She noticed how different this new neighborhood was. . . ." (with specific details added) or "He felt tense here, and knew it was because the unfamiliar area was so dark and isolated, with the great bulk of the mountains. . . ."

Having taken this step in viewpoint, don't forget the next: showing the character reaction as a result. This reaction might be shown in considerable detail, as the character slowly or swiftly goes through feelings about the new setting, then comes to thoughtful decisions designed to make everything feel better or safer again; at other times, showing how the character was reacting would be quite quick and simple.

In the above situation, for example, after showing the character's observation of the new setting (the different neighborhood), you might add three sentences like the following showing resultant immediate action and the beginning of a major character change (the immediate action and suggestion of character change italicized for clarity):

> She noticed how different the neighborhood was . . . how empty the streets, how shabby. Every black alleyway seemed like it might hide an attacker. She heard voices somewhere behind her. *She shivered and walked faster. Already she knew she was a different person here. She would never trust anyone again.* . . .

Sometimes, of course, it simply isn't practical for you to move your character to some drastically different physical setting in order to produce a desired character change. In such cases, however, it is often possible to keep the character in essentially the same setting, yet introduce significant alteration in that setting.

Any number of possibilities come to mind, and a few examples will help you see what I mean:

• When Jill opened her curtains onto the dear, familiar street, she immediately saw the big moving van next door, and the strange boxes being unloaded. . . .

• "Bill," the boss said, "we are going to redecorate your office to reflect the new duties I have in mind for you."

• Clouds scudded over the sun, and it began to rain. Marianne's depression began to grow. . . .

• The *Detour* signs went up Monday morning, and Ted's store was shut off from traffic.

The key to success in handling all such instances lies in locating the kind of change within the present setting that is most likely to jar the character and create the possibility and even the need for character change. Obviously, you must mix and match properly.

What do I mean by this? Well, look again at the examples

above. When Jill opens her curtains and sees boxes being unloaded from the van, she would possibly worry about that kind of change. Storekeeper Ted, however (in the fourth example), wouldn't worry about boxes being unloaded nearby, but the detour (which might not worry Jill) is a potentially disastrous change in *his* setting.

So you can change character by moving him to a new setting, or by introducing the right kind of changes in his present setting. That leaves the third basic way of using setting to change character, which is, essentially to leave the setting the same, but have the character notice new things about it.

One of the most obvious examples of this that I've ever seen involved a friend who had always been physically active and cheerful. One day he happened to fall and slightly injure his back. As a result of this minor injury, which at first had seemed frighteningly serious, he became more cautious and began looking for other possible dangers in his environment. He noticed floor tiles which might be slippery, pavement that was even slightly uneven, area rugs that might slip. He began to see every familiar staircase, escalator and change of floor level in the local mall as a place where he might fall again. He began to see almost everything in his familiar setting in a new way, and so he began *acting* in a new way, no longer taking walks or going out much by himself . . . finally becoming almost a recluse.

I'm happy to report that my friend went into therapy and managed to overcome the irrational fears that had made him see his setting in a new and dark way, which only fed those fears. Finally he saw quite clearly how the mechanism in his case had worked:

1. A sharp experience jolted him out of seeing things as he always had.

2. A growing alertness to a familiar setting, with his new orientation, caused him to notice things he had never noticed before.

3. Interpretation of the new things he noticed made him begin to act differently—he "became a different person," as he later put it.

This is the machinery by which you can get your character to experience his story setting in new ways, and so change as a result. You should first make something happen to get your character looking at his setting freshly, in a new light. You next show him finding "new" things in his setting (new to him, that is). Then you show him changing as a result.

In a few cases you might not even need a dramatic or sharp experience to get the ball rolling. Stories of boredom or desperation are quite common, and in many of them the character finally goes bonkers because *nothing* has changed in the setting, and seemingly never will. Once the character becomes aware of this dreadful unchangableness, then the very lack of change itself becomes a powerful potential instrument of character-change.

You can also use setting to create longer-term and more subtle character growth. Consider the change in the TV series character mentioned earlier, Dr. Joel Fleischman in *Northern Exposure*, over the first two seasons the show was on the air. At first he was in a panic and only wanted out of Cicely, the fictional town. Later, however, as he began to know people in the area and see some of the area's natural beauty, his attitude subtly changed and he became more human and forgiving. (Even his dress changed from modish New York to sloppy Alaskan bush pilot.) He became more calm and the hard edge of sarcasm dulled. Even later in the series, when he learned his forced stay in Alaska was to be longer than he had previously thought, he remained a man changed by his setting even as he bemoaned the fact. The setting's impact on his character, while slow in taking effect, is obvious.

This kind of interaction between character and setting almost always takes place, whether the writer designs it or simply allows it to happen. You should be as aware of it as possible, and use it to your advantage whenever you can.

SUGGESTED EXERCISE

As an exercise at this point, you may wish to write a short story segment in which you quite consciously delineate how a setting changes a character. Place yourself in the character's viewpoint and show him or her observing something about the setting, and reflecting on the observation. Then show, in viewpoint, that the character realizes he is seeing the setting in a different light. Define how his perception has changed, and, if possible, why it has changed. Finally, show the character reflecting on this changed attitude and wondering how the change is going to affect his plot motives and interaction with other characters.

Doing an exercise like this may feel mechanical. No matter. I urge you to do it, writing it step-by-step in the order I've just given you. I think the work will give you a better feel for how setting can have direct impact on character. The better you come to understand this interrelationship, the better you can tailor setting to character, and vice versa.

USE OF SETTING AS A CHARACTER

The tactic of making a setting into a character was mentioned previously in connection with my novel, *Twister*. It seems appropriate to reiterate the point in the context of this discussion. In short, the point is that sometimes a setting (or aspect of a setting) can be so overwhelmingly important in development of the plot (and the characters' lives) that it seems to take on a life of its own. This is a dynamic which cannot be forced; nothing could be cornier than trying to breathe life into a setting not vital and central enough to "take over" a story. But setting can become a character when setting, plot and characters blend perfectly.

In Arthur Hailey's *Hotel*, for example, the setting also becomes something of a character in its own right, practically taking on a life of its own. Similarly, in Hailey's *Airport*, the terminal building and everything it contains seems to become for the reader almost a huge living organism itself. In stories of the sea, the sea often becomes the central antagonist, and seems (even in a classic narrative poem like "The Rime of the Ancient Mariner") to become malevolent.

Clearly, setting and character are inextricably tied in the dynamic of fiction. But setting can affect fiction in other ways, too, as the next chapter describes.

CHAPTER 9

HOW SETTING ADDS TO STORY MEANING AND VITALITY

IN DESIGNING THE SETTING or settings for your story, it's important to remember that the setting, and how you handle it, may go far toward finally defining what your story means. In addition, your work on the setting may stimulate your imagination to explore story angles and ideas that weren't at all in your original concept of the tale.

STORY MEANING

Selection of setting can profoundly affect story meaning because some themes may be difficult or even impossible to examine in a certain kind of setting, while a different setting could make these same themes seem almost inevitable as a concern of the characters in such a place and time. If you begin planning your story to be played out in a rough, isolated wilderness setting, for example, that choice may at the outset be nothing more than a convenience for you, or the first idea that leaped into your mind. But selection of such a setting virtually eliminates some story themes and makes others likely.

For example, if you choose to set your story in a rugged, isolated mining town in the Klondike a century or more ago, it's hard to imagine that your story's meaning could have much to do with any of the following:

- The pressures of high society on a young woman's marriage plans
- The difficulty of choosing a college curriculum
- Country club exclusion due to racism
- The desperation of urban slums
- The choice of an apartment complex roommate
- Finding a date for the prom
- Lost airline tickets
- Harrassment by telephone calls
- Concern about AIDS
- Worry about environmental pollution and endangered wildlife.

The first six themes in this list relate to physical location of the setting. The situations listed would not likely exist in a place like the Klondike. The next three themes on the list relate to the time of the setting. Airlines, telephones and AIDS would not exist in a Klondike setting.

The last theme on the list, environmental pollution, would not be likely because of the attitude existing in such a setting: Until fairly recent times, environmental concerns were not much of a worry, and certainly old-time miners repeatedly raped the environment with no thought whatsoever of the consequences in pollution and destruction of wildlife. As a matter of fact, prevailing frontier attitudes toward wildlife were the opposite of today's; killing off all wolves, coyotes and bears was a positive value in those days.

So choice of a setting limits the themes you can deal with.

Conversely, choice of a setting immediately suggests themes which are possible. Using the same isolated, old-time Klondike setting, some possible ideas and themes come to mind at once:

- Greed for gold
- The threat of starvation in the wild
- The danger of wild animal attack
- The quest for food and shelter
- The value of friendship
- The terror of being lost in the wilderness
- Homesickness for civilization.

Once you realize this interdependence of setting and thematic ideas, you can better tailor your setting to your ideas. That wilderness setting might be chosen and developed consciously in order to state as clearly as possible a realized theme involving courage against great odds, perhaps, or the saving strength of religious faith in a time of isolation and trial. If you also emphasized certain other aspects of the wilderness—the cruel and random death of prey animals, as one illustration, or the seemingly hostile persistence of the killing winter gale—you might more clearly develop a theme about personal courage.

We often see this relationship between setting and meaning most clearly in movies, because so much has to be shown and not explained in words. In the *Treasure of Sierra Madre*, for example, the war between good and evil impulses in the characters is emphasized and made clearer because of the savage and primitive conditions under which the men exist, leaving little or no room for pretense or manners. The recent *Batman* movies derived part of their meaning from the dark, towering, crumbling city infrastructure that formed their setting. Many critics saw serious ideas about the human condition depicted in these films. The setting put the audience in a somber frame of mind, and gave outrageous activities a semblance of verisimilitude. Played in a less menacing and terrible urban setting, the stories might have been seen merely as comic book nonsense.

This relationship between setting and story meaning was brought home to me most vividly when I was writing a novel a few years ago titled *A Boat Named Death*. The story is of an old mountain man, quite mad, who stumbles upon a woman and her small children in a cabin in the wilderness. Through being touched by their total vulnerability and dependence on him to save their lives, he is changed from practically an animal to a love-filled man who faces his own death for the sake of others.

The novel met with some success, but probably could not have done so if the choice of setting had not been right. Most of the story is of the man's attempt to get the little family to medical help by taking them down a wild river in flood in an old rowboat with the word "Death" painted on its side. The trapper's struggle against the river—which seems to him a character bent on their annihilation — becomes a symbol of his entire life struggle, and explains how he became the man he is. But, at the same time, his journey down the river becomes a spiritual one, his heart changing as the river batters and almost destroys him. The setting, the boat in the careening river, makes possible the themes of man against nature, and man against himself. A final change in the setting, to a small and hostile town bent on the trapper's destruction, makes possible an emphasis on the trans-forming power of love, even on a man whom the wilds had prac-tically turned into a beast.

Every writer comes upon situations like this, where the choice of setting not only defines the kinds of ideas that can be explored, but suggests ways that all or part of that setting can be transformed into a symbol that contributes to story meaning. In an example earlier in this book, we used an old clock tower, visible from all over a small town. One immediately thinks of using the clock tower as a symbol for the passing of time, or for a town's living in the past as if time had stood still, or to illumi-nate the story's meaning.

In such ways, setting can have a profound impact on your story's meaning. You should be alert to this fact, and remember it in matching plot to character, and both to setting. In a proper blend of the three, a story meaning and depth of ideas will come much more clear. To put this another way, the perfect setting can make all the difference in what your story ultimately means.

You should also remember, however, that conscious manip-ulation of the setting and other story elements does not mean that you should set out on a mad quest for symbols and meta-phors in your setting. Symbolic meaning, when it occurs, is usu-ally an outgrowth of the creative process itself. Such meaning usually develops fully in your mind only as you write the story. It's very dangerous to set out on a piece of fiction with the idea of "making something a symbol." The result too often is artifici-ality.

What should you do, then? Simply remember that setting can affect meaning in the ways we have mentioned here. Work to make setting harmonious with your other fiction elements. If symbolic or metaphorical meaning comes clear to you as you write the story, consider ways you might point it out more clearly. But never force it; that way lies disaster.

STORY IDEAS

We've seen in earlier chapters how good setting makes the story world vital and vibrant and real to the reader. But there's also a quite different advantage of good setting: The impact it can have on the writer herself as she researches and creates her tale.

Many writers have experienced the "turn-on" that research digging can bring. What happens is that new and previously unsuspected facts turn up during the research, or some new detail or anecdote provides unexpected delight. In either case, the writer gets newly excited, and sometimes gets new story or character ideas from the experience. What can also happen is that the writer imaginatively gets so deeply into her setting as she writes, that she actually sees possibilities in it that were previously not seen.

The late Clifton Adams, one of our most gifted western writers mentioned earlier, told me once with great pleasure how he had stumbled upon a historical record of French foreign legionnaires actually assigned in south Texas during frontier times. This unusual historical sidelight so fascinated Cliff that he did considerably more research about it and found material for use in several later novels. Phyllis A. Whitney has remarked that she researched a setting for an adult suspense novel and found enough material for an additional young adult book. In my own career I have had numerous similar experiences: Medical research done for my novel *Halls of Dishonor* gave me considerable additional information about the medical setting, which was one of the inspirations for a later book called *Miracleworker*, another medical story. The germ of the plot for *Miracleworker*, as a matter of fact, came from an accidental encounter with a medical supply "detail man" (salesman) during a research visit for the other novel.

Careful research is required to make sure your setting is accurate and believable, as discussed back in chapter three. But

such research very often pays the considerable dividend of inspiring new ideas for setting, as well as indicating how story
people in such a setting might think and act, and how a plot in
such a setting might play out.

The moral? Never shirk research. Learn to love it. Even
when you think you have done enough research for your story
setting, try to dig just a little deeper—conduct that one more
interview, visit one more site, write one more letter or read one
more book on the subject. Trust the process of research. It will
feed your imagination in ways you may never have dreamed of.

You may indeed find that the inspiration continues through
the writing process, even after you thought learning about your
setting was finished. In a curious way, the process of writing
sometimes intensifies a writer's vision. In fact-writing, putting
the words on paper sometimes helps clarify the very thought
the writer is struggling to record. In fiction, it is even more
common for a writer to begin writing a description or factual
passage about a setting, and suddenly find herself imaginatively
transported into that setting in a more vivid way than was possible before she started writing it down.

So research provides inspiration, and writing down ideas
can help the imagination focus and crystalize the very imagining. The ideas form words and then the words, as they are written, clarify the ideas. It's a strange process and I don't begin to
understand it. I just know it happens, and very often it happens
when the writer is describing a setting, and suddenly finds herself so deeply immersed in that setting, in her imagination, that
she is amazed.

Try it. Write a detailed description of a setting you know a
lot about. Put down concrete physical details, emotion-packed
observations of feelings about the setting. As you write, you will
almost certainly find your imagination further stimulated by the
process itself.

Many writers, knowing how research and writing can fuel
the imagination, take the learning process a step further. They
become a fond joke among their friends because they always
seem to be making an unnecessary trip or going to a meeting
they don't have to attend, or starting with great vim and vigor

into some new hobby which their previous life gave no indication about.

Such writers do these things because they want to seek out new experience. They know you can never predict when such an experience might suggest an entirely new backdrop for a story. They also do these things because they have learned to love information for its own sake.

I admit to being one of those who constantly leaps into new hobbies. I have been at one time or another a photographer, a guitar player, a hunter, a fisherman, a private pilot, a camper, a ham radio operator, a golfer, a tennis player, a pigeon-raiser, a carpenter and a model train enthusiast. (And I've probably forgotten some hobbies that should be mentioned, too.) I went into each of these activities with enthusiasm, wanting to learn just as much about it as I could. I've had a great deal of fun. But I've also derived great benefits in terms of story settings because every specialty or hobby exists in its own arcane little world.

I think, for example, of standing in an airport hangar listening to pilots swap flying stories; there is a characteristic preoccupation here, and special lingo based on special shared skills and knowledge. Then I recall the days with amateur radio operators at events like the annual American Radio Relay League "Field Day," when operators set up in the out-of-doors to train for emergency situations; again the interests are unique, the people are unusual, and the lingo specialized. Each hobby's microworld has its own informal oral library of folk tales and jokes, some of which can stimulate your imagination with ideas for plots as well as settings.

Entering such a hobby world can bring all sorts of new information and ideas for story settings. And it can also be a lot of fun; such new experiences and learning keep you young . . . keep your brain nimble and eager.

In addition, your enjoyment of learning new things and meeting different kinds of people will help you maintain your enthusiasm, help keep your mind open to new experiences and ideas, and, quite simply, help you maintain a focus broader than your own private world of work and family.

This last point is very important, although it does not relate solely to the setting in your story. Writing is a lonely business, and it is all too easy to become so focused and intense about your work that you start closing doors and windows, turning down chances to meet new people, and begin to resemble a hermit. If your story world is to be vibrant and convincing, you must be out in the world, continually drawing from new and stimulating experiences. Research—and hobbies—make sure you maintain this outer focus.

A word should also be said about "painless research" of a different type: travel. As mentioned before in a different context, we tend to get so used to our everyday environment that we take many things for granted, and practically don't see them anymore. Familiarity breeds a kind of blindness. Traveling to a new locale, where nothing is familiar, awakens all the observational apparatus; we look, *really* look, at a church or store or office building that we might drive right by without seeing if it were in our humdrum, everyday setting. A change of scene sharpens all our observational skills. Even after we return home, we see things with fresh and inquisitive eyes for quite some time.

I'll talk about travel for on-site research of setting in Appendix 1 on research techniques as well as in chapter fifteen.

SUGGESTED SELF-EXAMINATION

Perhaps this chapter has suggested a course of self-examination that might help you analyze your own "research" and setting work in its broadest possible definition. Let me offer a few specific ideas for such a self-exam.

Look at the settings you have used in your last four stories or books. Are they very much the same? Are they small-town settings, for example, or all contemporary, or perhaps all big-city neighborhood or all business? If they are, ask yourself what other different setting you should research for your next creative effort.

Can you see many things that your settings have in common, even if they appear different on the surface? Do your story people always come from similar backgrounds, for example? Do they always have the same values? What different backgrounds or values could you research for your next setting?

Study the way you described physical settings in recent stories. Do you always stress what is seen, at the expense of mentioning other sense impressions? Is it possible you could enrich your descriptions if you took a trip or tried a new hobby which might excite your mind and make your observations—and writing—more acute?

Have you done as much research as you should have for recent stories? If not, why not? List ten sources of setting information you regularly use—or *should* be using. Have you taken an interesting trip, even a short one, in the last six months? Have you looked into or begun taking part in a new hobby in the last year? Think about these things!

Finally, one more exercise. Select a setting for a story which would be quite uncharacteristic for your work: a place and time and set of attitudes you have never used as a story backdrop before. Don't make this selection easy; pick something really "out in left field" in terms of what you usually do.

Now research this setting, and prepare a fact portfolio about it. Make up and fill out a setting research form for it. (You will find one writer's setting research form as an example in Appendix 2.)

This work is guaranteed to open your eyes to some of your tendencies about handling setting. It will also, I feel sure, stimulate you to find new ways to handle your setting problems.

CHAPTER 10

SETTING AND VIEWPOINT: IT'S HOW YOU LOOK AT IT

AT MANY POINTS IN THE TELLING OF A STORY, an author faces the decision of where to put the vantage point—the point from which the setting is to be described or discussed. Fundamentals concerning this decision were discussed in chapter two and mentioned again in chapter three. Let's briefly review those points and then look at other aspects.

Essentially, what you often have to decide, as the author of the piece, is where you stand—where you place the reader's imagination—in experiencing the story setting. In the broadest terms, you have the two choices already mentioned: The omniscient or author-objective panoramic view, told as a god might tell it, seeing everything and knowing virtually everything, or the view as experienced from inside a character, and limited to what that single character can realistically experience and know.

Each approach has its pros and cons. So let's reconsider them as briefly as possible.

THE OMNISCIENT VIEWPOINT

The omniscient approach offers three distinct advantages:

- It offers the broadest possible scope.
- It allows the author to provide information no character knows.
- It is economical—allows summary.

Useful in describing scenery, landscape, and great movements over time, the omniscient viewpoint allows you the author to show anything you wish from as far away, or as close, as you desire. It allows you to provide a long-time sense of history. Such "on high" observations can also include information that no character inside the story could possibly know. Therefore, the omniscient viewpoint has many applications in broad-sweep situations.

Such a viewpoint is not used only in broad-sweep situations, however. It is a very efficient way of showing information about a setting, and allows for summary because you the author are not stuck in the lifelike narrative of a story character, whose experience often must be told moment-by-moment, with no summary, in order to be as realistic as possible. That's why you sometimes find a writer getting out of character viewpoint at the start of a story segment in order to provide a few broad brushstrokes of setting as quickly as possible. In such situations, the omniscient viewpoint is the most effective.

Here, for example, is a brief use of the technique by novelist Jeff Clinton in a recent western titled *Big Sky Revenge*:

> Night came, and with it a clear starry sky and the sliver of a rising moon. The ground quickly gave off its heat and in the dark it was cold, the kind of cold that sinks quickly to the bone.

This is economical writing. A broad and general picture of the setting is provided in fewer words than might have been necessary if the same description were put in the viewpoint of a character, who might have had to walk outside and look around, shiver, etc., in order to experience the same thing. The brief passage also illustrates the ability to summarize. At least an hour passes in two sentences. If told from a character's viewpoint, the passage of so much time could hardly have been summarized so deftly because there is no summary in real life, and little in the lives of fiction characters; rather, the writer would have had to add considerable minute details in order to show time passing, rather than simply summarizing it, as the omniscient approach allows.

Just as the technique has advantages of sweep and compression, however, it has disadvantages which you must weigh before making a decision to use it:

- You may lose your character identification.
- You may get carried away and overdescribe.

Since omniscient writing by definition is told outside a character viewpoint, there is always the danger that the reader may lose contact with the viewpoint character if such passages go on very long. Your shifting to a broad, godlike viewpoint takes your reader to that mountaintop or place out of space and time, too, remember. He may stop thinking about your main story character and her outlook during such on-high journeys. Such a loss of contact with the viewpoint character may mean loss of reader sympathy and identification with that character—and, consequently, loss of interest in the human story.

To put this another way, there is a danger that such a passage, if extended very long, will turn the reader's attention from the story people to the setting exclusively, and all storytelling will be lost as the reader studies a kind of stop-action photograph in words. Make sure the advantages clearly outweigh dangers such as this one if you "go omniscient."

The other disadvantage noted above—that one might get carried away in omniscience—is easier to deal with once you realize the danger exists. Sometimes a writer gets so deeply into the broad-scale imagining that she is carried away and starts putting in great gobs of purple prose. Or she may start lecturing the reader about the facts.

I think most of us have cringed at one time or another when encountering an awful purple patch of overheated description in a story. Perhaps most of us have almost dozed off, too, when confronted by a huge block of solid factual information that stopped the story dead in its tracks. Almost always such errors come when the writer is in an omniscient mode. Always keep in mind the reactions of your readers.

THE RESTRICTED VIEWPOINT

What should we remember about using the restricted viewpoint of a story character as our place for viewing the setting? Again there are advantages and disadvantages you may already be aware of from the earlier discussions in chapters two and three. Here we'll review and then move on. (You may wish to return to the earlier chapters as part of your study here.)

The advantages of viewpoint restriction:

- It's convincing because it gives the reader this information the same way he experiences real life: from the limited view of a lone individual.
- It's simpler because there will always be many aspects of the setting that the single individual cannot sense or know— being on the wrong side of the mountain to see the waiting outlaws, for example, or standing too far from the scene of the crash to hear the clashing of metal.
- It tends to be briefer because a character caught up in the action and problems of your story ordinarily just won't have the time to notice a lot of things.

We've looked in earlier chapters at the major disadvantages of restricted viewpoint, and need only mention them by way of review here:

- There may be times when you want to show a broader picture, and simply can't find a character who could experience all that.
- There may be information you want to provide that no single character could possibly know.

THE URGE TO TELL TOO MUCH

I've known writers who got very uneasy—or downright panicky—because they thought they needed to get certain broad-scale information or sense impressions into their story at a given point, but couldn't find a character to experience all that they desired to convey. If you ever get that feeling, let me suggest that you sit back for a minute and ask yourself if the reader really needs that panoramic view (or additional information). Often you may discover that she doesn't, and that your feeling is an *author* concern, not a *reader* concern. You may be wanting to tell more than necessary just because you happen to know it.

It's hard sometimes to accept that a reader doesn't need to experience or know something. You know everything about the setting, can see it all in your imagination, and your natural impulse is to want to share your vision with your reader—to put in everything for the reader to know, see, hear, smell, taste, feel and believe about the setting at that moment of story time. It's a brave impulse, and one that's very hard to dissuade writers of sometimes, but nearly always it's fallacious.

Your reader seldom needs to know all you do at any point. You might think he would benefit from a vast and panoramic view of that city setting, but he does not experience his real life that way, and he does not want to experience the story setting that way, either. Belief comes from identification with the viewpoint. Identification with the viewpoint comes from a restricted view of the setting. The reader's concern is with what the character knows. Your authorial concern about showing the big picture often has nothing whatsoever to do with telling a good story in the most effective way.

However, if you decide after reflection that broad-scale information is vital to the reader, you obviously may elect to assume the omniscient view for a short time. Or you may elect to keep your viewpoint limited to a single person at a time, but hop around among several characters in order to show what each is experiencing.

Let me offer one example here of how the omniscient viewpoint can provide a sweeping picture. This is from an early segment of the novel by Jeff Clinton mentioned earlier, *Big Sky Revenge*:

> It was a magnificent day: brilliant blue sky, a few low clouds forming a silvery haze on the lower slopes, the upper reaches already blinding white under their winter coat.

Crossing a swift stream, its banks encrusted with ice, Ford spooked an elk—a flash of tan and orange—in the long declivity a quarter-mile behind his house, on higher ground. He didn't fire. He saw some deer, a doe and a buck, higher up and at some distance. The light snow under the trees was crisscrossed with the tracks of rabbits, beavers, otters, and skunks. Ford walked steadily, his breath a huge cloud around him, and reached the turning in the creek designated on Craddock's map. He moved on.

A brief analysis of this short passage may be helpful. The passage comes after a transition in time, clearly marked by double white spaces in the text, so the reader presumably begins reading without too strong a thought connection to any viewpoint.

But even if circumstances make it possible for a switch to omniscience here, why does the author choose to use it? I think the answer is clear. Especially in an outdoor story of the Old West like this one, a feeling for the vastness of the country and its visual beauty are vital elements. The reader yearns imaginatively to see the mountains. And, as in virtually any story, he needs a periodic recontact with the physical setting to remind him of his physical orientation. Therefore, in this example, the author meets reader needs by "fleshing out" the setting with a panoramic view, and he takes advantage of a natural transition point to do so.

Notice, however, that the purely omniscient view is not maintained for long. The character Ford's name is mentioned midway in the second sentence. The fact that his name is mentioned does not in itself establish his viewpoint, because the godlike observer can see him just like he sees the mountains and snow. But mention of the character's name begins to set the reader up for insertion into a character viewpoint, and sure enough, two short sentences later, a viewpoint is established with the words *He saw*. Only Ford can know what he saw. Therefore, when these words occur, the reader is again placed in Ford's viewpoint.

You might also notice, however, that considerable material not necessarily in Ford's viewpoint follows this single viewpoint identifier. The light snow, Ford's heavy breathing, and all the rest of it contain no intrinsic evidence that they are from Ford's restricted viewpoint. So additional panoramic material is inserted. But a reader, once put into a viewpoint, will invariably tend to assume that everything which follows is experienced by that viewpoint. So here the additional panoramic material is assumed to be from Ford's viewpoint, and author Clinton is careful to make sure that nothing that comes later in this segment is from a viewpoint that the character Ford could not possibly experience. Clinton seems to know well one of the cardinal rules about handling point of view in setting as noted in chapter two. To state it negatively: Once in a viewpoint in any given segment, don't get back out of it.

A BRIEF RESTATEMENT

A brief restatement of the principles mentioned here and in earlier chapters relating to the subject of viewpoint may be in order.

• Use the "on high" omniscient viewpoint to establish general story setting, tone, the look and feel and possibly background of a place.
• Move inside a viewpoint character to gain reader identification, and to reflect character outlook and mood.
• Move from viewpoint character to "on high," if you must, at the beginning of segments, after a transition of some kind.
• Return to character viewpoint at the earliest opportunity.
• Always think about what the reader needs to know, not what you may know or want to inflict on the poor soul for no good reason.

If you follow these principles, your story setting will be presented fully, vibrantly and convincingly. But your job in handling your viewpoint will not be done. What's left? Pegging your presentation of setting to *feeling* and *mood*. Which is the subject of chapter eleven.

CHAPTER 11

SETTING THE MOOD: HOW SETTING VIEWPOINT CREATES ATMOSPHERE

BACK IN CHAPTER SIX WE BRIEFLY CONSIDERED emotional focus of a character as a unifying factor in storytelling, and promised to get back to the matter at an appropriate time. Having looked at viewpoint in chapter ten, we can now look more carefully at emotional focus and story mood, and how both interact with your story's setting.

It may be that you will choose to open your story, or relate parts of it, from the broad, omniscient viewpoint. In such situations, you still need to be conscious of the general emotional mood you wish your story to evoke in your reader; you will need to select details designed to create or enhance that general mood, be it joyfulness, sadness, fear, dread, anger, or whatever. More often, however, you will probably tell virtually all your story from the viewpoint of a character inside the story action, as discussed in chapter ten. In these cases, it is even more critical that you understand how the viewpoint affects story mood.

Your character's emotional set and the general mood conveyed by a story at any given point are inextricably bound together. Given a central character who is sad and lonely, for example, the depiction of the setting must reflect details generally in keeping with that mood, even if you happen to be writing from an omniscient viewpoint at the moment. When you are in character viewpoint, the need to dovetail character emotion and story mood is much more vital.

If you walk your sad and lonely viewpoint character into a bright and happy setting, the story mood will not be bright and happy despite the objective nature of the setting because your sad and lonely character will not see the setting in terms other than his own internal emotional set. Thus, walking into a joyful wedding, for example, he will see it all as a contrast to his own plight; you the author must show that the happiness around him only reminds him of his own sadness.

Three crucial aspects — *who* the story is about, *what* you show about the setting, and *how* everything feels to the reader — must be consistent in mood and reinforce one another. Your viewpoint character, like people in the real world, will interpret the setting through the lens of his current emotions. If you want to write a story with a sad and lonely mood, you will write about a character whose feelings are sad and lonely. If you write about a character whose feelings are sad and lonely, then your setting will look (or be interpreted as) sad and lonely because your viewpoint is that of a character who cannot interpret things in any other way.

Once you have recognized this dynamic interaction, you can consciously manipulate your story elements to give the story exactly the general mood you desire.

In writing any story, you need to think about the following generalized questions, all of which are closely linked:

- How do you want the reader to feel while experiencing the story?
- What is the general mood you hope to convey from the setting?
- How do your character's emotions color what he sees?
- What setting details impact both the character's feelings and general mood of the story?

Every story, you see, elicits a general feeling matrix in its reader. The poet T.S. Eliot, writing about this subject years ago, talked about what he called "the objective correlative," that precise relationship between what is presented and how it makes the reader feel. No story should leave the reader emotionally unmoved, or thinking, "So what?" Your setting must fit the desired feeling or your story won't work. So consciously analyzing how you want your reader to feel will help you plan and present your setting.

You attain this reader feeling through story mood. If you want your reader to feel sadness, for example, you need to present your story in a setting which includes somber details, unhappy elements, dark shades of gray, items designed to create a mood that will lead to the desired feeling.

And how will your character's emotions color what is shown of the setting? We have already seen how a happy character might "reach out" into his environment and notice happy things, while a sad one is likely to notice the sad, or interpret whatever he sees in a sad way. You can't simply depict a sorrowful setting, for example, without making sure that your character's feelings are such that sad details are what he will see because of the sorrowful tint to the emotional lenses through which he experiences the story world.

And what kind of details do you need in your setting to reinforce the desired mood? If the story is to leave the reader angry and resentful about some wrong in society, and if the mood is to be somber and bitter, and if the character is to be hurt and rejected, what specific details do you have to locate and present in the setting to make sure the character—and through him the reader—gets the desired feeling clearly and forcefully?

Sometimes, of course, a particular setting virtually demands a certain kind of emotional response in the character, a certain story mood, a certain reader feeling. A graveyard, for example, is difficult to imagine as a setting for a lighthearted, humorous story. Yet Peter S. Beagle achieved exactly this effect in his novel, *A Fine and Private Place*, through the viewpoint of an extremely unusual character. But Beagle's story is the exception which tends to prove the rule. More often than not, you should give some serious thought to the kinds of feeling a particular setting can predictably engender, and then make your setting decisions accordingly.

But general thoughtfulness and planning will not necessarily get the whole job done for you in terms of emotion and mood.

Your general questioning invariably must get down to specifics like some of the following:

1. In the opening of your story—What aspect of the setting should be shown at the earliest possible moment in the story to establish an opening mood or tone? What specific details should be included in this opening? From what vantage point should the opening be presented?

2. During the course of your story—What central unifying aspect of the setting should be shown repeatedly? What different views or experiences of this central aspect will be used to avoid obvious repetition? What other aspects of setting will be developed, and in what order?

How many different viewpoints will be employed? If settings change drastically, how will each new setting be established, and with what mood or tone?

If different viewpoint characters are to experience the setting, how specifically does each character's emotional outlook color his or her individual experience of the setting?

How will all differing views and aspects of the setting be unified in a coherent, consistent story mood or tone, and how do you want this general tone or mood to make the reader feel?

3. In the ending of your story, what feeling do you want to leave your reader with? What aspect of setting will you stress as the ending to help evoke this mood? From what viewpoint will this last look at setting be shown? Is there a possibility of developing story theme more clearly through employment of the closing look at setting?

Many of these questions are intimately interrelated, of course, but let's try to separate them and consider them individually insofar as it is possible.

STORY OPENING

In deciding what general aspect of the setting should be shown to establish a story-opening mood or tone, it is important to remember that the opening feeling you engender in your reader sets up his expectations for everything that follows. You need to be quite sure what mood you wish to evoke right from the outset.

Here we are talking about the broadest possible definition of mood, such as sadness, fear, joy, apprehension, isolation or engulfment. Every story *feels* a certain way, and this is what you need to define. Then, having defined it in your own mind as clearly as you can, you need to think about your setting and decide what you should present first to make the story feel that way to your reader right from the outset.

Perhaps you have envisioned a large city with teeming traffic, streets alive with business people during the daytime and crime at night; rivers, trains, air traffic, skyscrapers and large wooded parks; rich neighborhoods and poor ones. If the tone or mood of your story is to relate somehow to the dynamism of all this humming activity and the nervous electricity of a complex city environment, perhaps your opening should stress all of these aspects in a broad-view look written in a staccato style that adds to the electricity and confusion. On the other hand, if your story is really the sad and nostalgic tale of a couple growing old in Brooklyn, perhaps your focus at the outset will be as narrow as the description of a single potted violet on a windowsill behind the dusty front window of an upstairs apartment.

Suppose you opt for this second example. What other details besides the little potted plant will you show? A roach crawling on the glass or a small, silver-framed photo of a young serviceman killed in Vietnam? An old lamp with fringed shade on the marble-top table or the latest issue of *Penthouse*, folded open to the letters section? An unopened letter or an old-style telephone ringing? The distant scent of sachet or the stale odor of marijuana? Harsh street sounds or the soft sound of a recorded string quartet? Obviously, the specific details you choose will immediately serve to begin establishing your desired opening mood.

Also in terms of your opening there is the question of viewpoint. As discussed in chapter ten, description from the omniscient view is best accepted by the reader at times when a character viewpoint is not firmly in the reader's mind. Cer-

tainly the prime time when this is true is in the very opening
of the story. For that reason, you may well choose to begin
with an omniscient viewpoint and only later go into a character
viewpoint. It is also true that writers very often wish to establish a broad setting picture at the outset of the story, before
narrowing their focus, so this too may dictate an "on high"
viewpoint at the start.

Your desire for a particular mood, however, may suggest
the immediate presentation of setting from the viewpoint of a
character. If, for instance, the emotional mood of the central
character is vital to the feeling of the story throughout, you
might plunge your reader into that character's viewpoint (which
is to color everything) at once.

As an example, compare and contrast the following opening
lines of a story about a lonely person living alone in a squalid
setting. What is the general story feeling conveyed by this:

> A cold, steady rain pounded the deserted streets of the
> neighborhood, making the chill night more bleak and
> lonely. An old man in a dark raincoat hurried along the
> crumbling sidewalks and vanished into the shabby yellow
> light of a tavern on the corner. A police car trundled slowly
> through the dark, its headlights yellow, like the eyes of a
> great cat. . . .

As opposed to this:

> She bit her lip to keep from screaming. The pounding
> of the rain on the window of her small room was driving
> her mad. The night outside mirrored her feelings: black-
> ness . . . desolation. Fighting back tears, she watched an old
> man in a dark raincoat hurry along the deserted sidewalk
> and enter the corner bar. Another derelict, she thought in
> despair, another loser like me, waiting to die. Her head
> throbbed with pain. She felt nauseated. She looked at the
> bottle of blue pills on the cheap plastic end table, knowing
> they offered what she wanted most: oblivion . . . death.

Clearly the mood evoked by these two openings is quite different. One is from the omniscient viewpoint and establishes a dark, lonely, brooding, and perhaps threatening feeling in the setting. The second is *deeply* in a character viewpoint, so that the setting is as much inside her head as anywhere in the outside world. The mood that's established is in contrast with the first example, here being more desperate, anguished, miserable and limited.

What decisions will you make about your opening? Remember that you will be establishing reader expectations that you should be ready to meet with consistency in your handling of setting throughout the rest of the story. What you set up, you must follow through on.

STORY MIDDLE

Which brings us to the main course of your story, and some of the questions you have to consider for its progress.

As noted above, selection of a central unifying aspect of the setting is almost always a "must." Earlier we looked at setting up an old clock tower as such a unifier. What aspect will you select? Will it be a specific thing like the clock tower, or a more general repeated emphasis on setting, such as its isolation, or its place in the mountains or near the ocean shore?

It's important to avoid reader boredom as you return again and again to this central aspect of setting, so it will pay off if you plan carefully all the different ways you might refer to it. Can you describe or present it from differing locations which present different angles of view? From different viewpoints? Different times of day? Different emotional or intellectual perspectives? You will find it useful to plan some of these different approaches, making notes on how and when you might use them, including notations on how they will appear different to the reader, and perhaps the kind of wording that might be used.

Again using the clock tower as a basis for an example, the beginning of your brief and preliminary list of different ways of describing setting might look something like this:

Clock tower —

Seen from street below; from window across street; from edge of town; in noon sunlight; lighted at night; on city stationery masthead; from passing car a block away; possibly from private aircraft?

Vantage points to include omniscient, viewpoint of Stephanie and Roger.

Omniscient vantage-point descriptions objective but evocative of small-town, the great age of the tower, the town's parochialism. Stephanie sees tower as dear, familiar, reassuring, always nostalgic, happy. Roger, however, sees it with anger, resentment, a symbol of how the town holds Stephanie so she won't go away with him.

There will, of course, be many other details and aspects of the setting which will be presented during the course of your story. You need to know what most of these will be, so that setting references come instantly to your mind as you follow your character's journey through the plot. (It can badly slow down your plotting if you have to pause often in the first draft in order to think up what bit of setting detail should be inserted. If you know the details in advance, you will tend to drop them in quickly, without being distracted from your plot and character by the need to dream up something about the setting on the spur of the moment.)

Naturally, if your story is going to move into several settings, you need to do this kind of planning for each of them. As you do, you will find yourself beginning to see each from various viewpoints, and this will improve your imaginative connection with both your characters and your story world.

STORY ENDING

Little needs to be said about questions like those mentioned above, because most of the points involved have already been touched upon in the context of earlier story development. It should be noted, however, that the concluding feeling or mood conveyed by your setting may be almost as important as the opening one because this is the emotional hook on which you hang the entire tale—the feeling you hope to leave with your reader at the story's conclusion. It may or may not be precisely the feeling that you established at the outset. In a story of any length, it will have changed subtly because something has changed in the course of the story—events have taken place, characters' lives have been altered. For this reason, your characters are not likely to see their setting at the end of the story exactly as they saw it at the outset; their feelings have changed and they will see the setting differently, too.

So don't mechanically assume the end mood will be exactly as it was at the outset. It may be close, but some variation, some dramatic progress, nearly always will have taken place.

Finally, consider the possibility that some part of your setting—the clock in the old tower, for example once more—might ultimately be made to mean more than anyone realized it meant earlier in the story. Is it possible that your character, in the ending, suddenly sees the inexorable movement of the giant minute hand as the moments of her life slipping away? Does the tolling of the hour become the tolling of the bell "for thee," as in John Donne's poem which concludes, "Send not to see for whom the bell tolls,/ It tolls for thee." Or can the crumbling bricks of the tower come to be a metaphor for the crumbling dreams of your characters?

ALL SETTING IS EMOTIONAL IN PART

From all this you can draw an obvious conclusion: No mention of setting in fiction can be said to be wholly objective. Selection of viewpoint, as well as selection of the emotional lens through which the described place or event is seen, must be made with constant reference to the desired emotional feel of the story, its present plot situation, and the characters at the time of description.

Obviously, you need to plan carefully in this entire area. It's planning that will pay off in consistency of story mood and maximum impact on your reader.

CHAPTER 12

SHOWING SETTING DURING MOVEMENT AND ACTION

MOST OF THE TIME UP UNTIL NOW, we have been tacitly assuming that your handling of setting was being done in a kind of stop action—that you could present or describe setting details in relatively static terms. In writing fiction, however, you often confront situations where you have to show a character movement into a new setting, or where the action is swift enough that you can't realistically "stop to describe," and must get the job done on the fly, while things are happening. In this chapter we'll consider such common situations.

It's possible that you may be able to stand back in the omniscient mode to reorient the reader to a change in setting, or even rapid character movement through setting details. If you are moving the character into a new setting at a time of transition, as at the opening of a chapter, you of course have the option of doing an "on high" omniscient introduction, then moving into viewpoint. In such situations, principles we've already discussed will see you through the transitions involved. More often than not, however, you may find yourself already in a character viewpoint during such times of change. Then, you have to stay in viewpoint and at the same time show as much broad detail as possible in order to reorient the reader.

STAYING IN VIEWPOINT WHILE MOVING

The thing you have to remember in such cases is that your viewpoint character is probably in movement, and has other things beside the setting on his mind. Therefore, for the sake of realism, you must carefully pick broad-brush details that will stand for the whole setting, evocative brushstrokes that you can paint in a very few words because the character can't stop and "notice things for you" endlessly.

In such cases, ask yourself the following questions:

• What two or three broad details will best suggest the new setting to the reader?

• How can I capsulize these details in a few sharply evocative words?

• What is my character's preoccupation right now — what is he probably concerned with, in terms of the plot, which might color his perception of the new setting?

• What is my character's mood right now, and would this likely color his perception of the new setting?

Here is an example of a chapter opening written with these questions in mind. It's from a recently completed novel of mine, *Double Fault*. (Tor Books, New York, © Jack M. Bickham.)

The cosmic question (Brad Smith Faces Life, Chapter 600) was answered for me when my flight into Los Angeles was delayed several hours and I didn't clear the airport until almost 1 A.M.: I would not call Beth tonight.

In the morning there was nothing much to do around my motel in Burbank, and I could have called her at her office. I didn't, and this time there was no handy excuse. She would ask why I was in LA and I didn't like lying to her but telling her the truth would only restart the disagreement that had already begun to feel old.

There would be time to call her later during my visit, I told myself.

Whether I would do it or not was a question still occupying a part of my mind early that afternoon when I drove toward Whittier and the tennis club where the FBI report said Barbara Green always played tennis on Thursday.

It was a hot day and the air quality wasn't very good. I couldn't see the mountains. The sun looked like a big silver cottonball through the heat-haze. Traffic on the freeway was dense as always. I watched my mirror, but saw no signs of being followed. In the traffic, that meant nothing. This entire mission seemed to me today to be a classic waste of time. I tried to convince myself that I was just feeling sorry for myself because of the simmering anger at Beth, the continuing erosion of hope.

The Redlands Racquet Club turned out to be a medium-sized facility parked behind the palm trees and lush grass of a municipal golf course. The builders had tried to make it look like San Simeon, or maybe an old-time movie theater. I found a parking place among the glittering Toyotas and Volvo station wagons — mommy's day at the club, children — and went in with my racket bag slung over one shoulder and my duffel over the other.

I hoped for an observation deck, the better to spot her and stage our "accidental" encounter, and I was not disappointed. Walking out onto the utility-carpeted upper deck, I had a nice view of the sixteen courts, cement with green plastic paint, all in use. For a few seconds, scanning, I didn't see her.

Then I did: out on Court 8, two women slugging it back and forth in a singles match far more vigorous than any of the games on nearby courts; a tall, lithe, leathery blonde in pink, blasting every ball with a controlled ferocity, and Barbara — a slender, pretty brunette with a red headband and graceful oncourt movements that made it appear she never had to hurry to make a return. Thank you, FBI. You have done good and now my deception can begin. I looked for the staircase that would take me down to court level.

The problem I faced in this segment was how best to handle a transition in both space and time, from the character Brad Smith's home near Missoula, Montana, to Los Angeles, after a day's air travel. Needed: the speediest possible setting change that would reorient the reader, leaving him feeling comfortable in the changed story environment.

First I selected the two or three broad details about the southern California setting that I thought would "say Los

Angeles" to the reader in a few words. I picked *hot weather*, *smog* and *heavy freeway traffic*.

In terms of time reorientation, I decided simply to mention the time of day or night without resorting to such tricks as showing clocks or having a character reset his watch.

This still left the question as to what familiar attitudes, feelings, character preoccupations or physical objects I might use to show the reader that some things were the same although the physical setting had changed. In this case I chose the character Brad's habitual glum preoccupation with his friend Beth, and the deterioration of their relationship.

The first paragraph thus mentions Brad's characteristic preoccupation immediately ("The cosmic question," etc.). The remainder of the sentence establishes both place and time in a factual way: "It is now later, dear reader, and we are in Los Angeles."

The second paragraph continues to focus on the preoccupation, moves the setting to a Burbank motel, and changes the time setting to the next day. The third brief paragraph is a bridge designed to move the character — and the reader — off the preoccupation for the moment in order to let the story proceed on another line. The fourth paragraph changes the time setting again, this time to afternoon, and puts Brad in a car moving from the motel setting to a tennis club setting.

Paragraph five, beginning "It was a hot day" is the one designed to put the reader more concretely into the new physical setting. Here the selected broad details — heat, smog and traffic — are inserted. Brad's emotions are shown as another help to the reader, to keep him feeling he is on familiar emotional turf during this setting change.

Then the picture of setting is narrowed from the broad Los Angeles area to the specific tennis club. Again, suggestive details are used rather than a detailed description, and the character is kept on the move.

The following paragraph, beginning "I hoped for an observation deck," again narrows the focus of setting, this time to a specific part of the club, and shows the character's motive for making this move inside the setting. Finally, at the very end, he reaches his new specific place in the setting, and the stage is set for interaction with other characters to resume.

Note the specific wording and phraseology designed to make the new setting as vivid as possible with the fewest suggestive words, and at the same time to keep place movement and time defined. Some of those specifics include the following:

- didn't clear the airport until 1 A.M.
- in the morning
- around my motel in Burbank
- early that afternoon
- drove toward Whittier
- hot day and the air quality wasn't very good
- couldn't see the mountains
- sun looked like a big silver cottonball through the heat haze
- traffic on the freeway was dense
- Redlands Racquet Club
- medium-sized facility
- parked behind the palm trees and lush grass
- San Simeon
- glittering Toyotas and Volvo station wagons
- my racket bag and duffel
- observation deck
- sixteen courts, cement with green plastic paint.

Please understand that I don't offer this excerpt as a particularly wonderful piece of scene-transition work, but as one that might be instructive. As with most of the illustrations in this book, my own work is used as illustration because I can at least tell you what I was thinking when it was written. And here my memory of the transition problem, and how I chose to work it out, is quite fresh.

The brief approach used in the excerpt you've just studied will work equally well from first person or third person perspective, and from a limited or a broad, "on-high" viewpoint. The overriding concern you the writer should have with scene transitions is clarity: The danger of reader confusion is serious at such times, and so is the danger of losing your story movement. Brevity, and new plot development as soon as possible, will help you avoid loss of forward movement. Key broad details, shown vividly, will help provide quick reorientation for the reader. Remembering your character's mood or preoccupation will help the reader stay oriented to the continuing problems which the change in setting do not alter.

With awareness of these principles and a bit of practice, I think you'll find such transitions becoming easier to handle.

DESCRIBING SETTING DURING SWIFT ACTION

A more difficult problem with setting can come when there is rapid character movement inside the general setting, or when the setting itself is changing with great speed (as when a storm is developing, for example). Most such situations occur within the body of a chapter or section, after you have established a character viewpoint. Telling the reader everything he needs to know during such rapid action is a challenge to any writer in terms of clarity and brevity.

To help you handle these situations, remember that your viewpoint character will be preoccupied with the action and therefore able to catch only fleeting, dominant impressions and sense images. Detailed description will be out of the question.

In planning and writing such a sequence you must keep yourself imaginatively wholly within the viewpoint, seeing only what the character sees, hearing only what he hears, and so forth. A danger during very rapid change in setting, or character movement through the setting, is loss of contact with the viewpoint. In other words, the movement may be so swift and exciting that you the writer may slip, in your own excitement, and include setting observations that the viewpoint character could not know. You must work hard to immerse yourself deeply in the viewpoint, and deal only with what he can possibly experience.

You must remember also that the viewpoint character will often experience setting impressions that are fragmentary and confusing; the source of a sound may be unknown, for example, or various impressions may seem to crash in simultaneously and confusingly. Don't worry if fragmentary impressions seem confusing. Your character may be confused, and if so, that's precisely the view of the story environment you want to portray.

Broad, dominant impressions may be all the character can experience at the moment. At time of such rapid movement, your character realistically won't have time to notice a great many fine details. Therefore, you must content yourself with including only the dominant, overwhelming impressions—all the character could realistically be expected to take in.

Strong action verbs will help carry the reader swiftly along with the movement. At all times of rapid movement in the setting, one of your aims as a writer is to convey that movement not only in what you show, but how you show it. Nothing can kill the sense of swift movement more surely than passive verbs or weak, limping sentences. You must strive for the strongest possible action wording.

Any descriptive segment must be extremely brief. There is never time for much description at such times. A pause to describe something can destroy the very sense of speed you must convey.

The character's reaction to the setting stimulus may be more important to the reader than the actual stimulus, but you have to show the setting stimulus or the reaction won't make sense. What happens in the setting at times of high action may not be nearly as important as your character's impressions of it and its impact on him. Is that loud bang a gunshot or a car backfiring, or possibly a firecracker? No matter; if identifying the source ruins the story, then the viewpoint can't know, so you *can't* tell. What's important is that the sound makes the character jump and run to the window to look outside. So you must always focus on the result inside the character.

Here's an example of a rapid-fire action sequence using these principles. It's also from *Double Fault*:

Running outside to his rented Taurus, he glanced south and saw that the Buick had already vanished around a slight turn in the highway where it started to ascend into the foothills. He grabbed his door handle and almost broke some fingers, forgetting he had locked up. Getting the key in the lock and jumping inside took another few precious seconds. Backing out seemed to take an eternity.

Floorboarding the Taurus's accelerator, he swung onto the pavement and headed in the direction the Buick had taken. Startled faces looked up from an open-air vegetable stand as he rocketed past them, the Ford's transmission screaming in protest at such violent treatment. *All I need is for the town constable or somebody to arrest my ass for speeding.*

Reaching the curve where the Buick had vanished, he had to ease off a bit and allow the transmission to upshift. Then he poured power to the engine again, and it responded sweetly, the speedometer going up around *70.*

Ahead — well ahead, too far ahead — Davis could see the Buick nearing the outskirts of town, brake lights flaring brightly in the evening gloom, then swinging to the right and off the highway. He kept standing on the gas until he was almost on top of the place where the Buick had turned, seeing only at the last second that the intersecting road was gravel. He swayed violently onto the gravel, half-losing it as the back end slewed around, then catching control again and pouring on more power. The guy in the Buick with Brad had turned on his headlights, which made two nice red tail-light signals for Davis to watch for. He kept his lights out to avoid detection if possible.

The gravel road swung through a series of curves and came out in the deep canyon of a shallow river off to Davis's left. He was having a bad time seeing the road in the dimness without headlights. A pale cloud of whitish powder put in the air by the Buick ahead didn't help matters.

Sweat stung Davis's eyes. He was walking a tightrope, and knew it: get too close, and the bald man would realize he was being followed and possibly kill Brad — if he hadn't already done so; fall too far back in an over-abundance of caution, on the other hand, and you could lose him altogether. Davis took several gravel curves in controlled drifts, and was rewarded with a glimpse of the Buick tail-lights well ahead. The bastard was driving like a maniac.

Which he probably was, Davis thought. Davis hadn't had time to see much, but he had seen enough to know that the driver of the car ahead fit the sketchy description he had of the conspirator who was still at large.

What did he want with Brad? Revenge? If so, for what? Far more likely, he had learned somehow that Brad might know where Kevin Green was. But how could abducting Brad help the loony in any way — abduction being far and away the best Davis could assume this was?

Sheer red rock walls closed in tightly on the road, which had begun to get worse, narrower and washboarded by traffic and erosion. Ahead was a tighter curve to the right around an outcropping of the hundred-foot rock face. Davis eased off a little and then swung wide into the turn. At the last possible instant he spotted the yellow glare of headlights just around the bend somewhere. Jamming his weight hard on the brake, he spun the wheel and felt for an instant that he was losing the Taurus altogether.

Dirt flew around the windows as the Ford skidded, swinging over jagged bumps in the dirt. Davis spun the wheel the opposite direction and got a semblance of control just as he went into the deepest part of the curve. A little Jeep, headlights yellow, poked its snout around the turn ahead of him. It immediately veered right as far as it could go without hitting the shoulder dropoff into the streambed. Davis took the Taurus back right, over-correcting as he regained full control and hitting the gravel shoulder nearest the cliff face. The right side of the Taurus brushed the rock wall with an ugly crunching sound, and then Davis was free again and speeding on into the thicker dust-cloud left by the Jeep.

The dirt road narrowed and straightened out for several hundred yards, paralleling the rocky stream on the left. Davis didn't see any sign of the Buick's tail-lights ahead. Gritting his teeth so hard they ached, he floorboarded the accelerator again, making the Ford leap anxiously into passing gear as the tach needle swung into the red.

Another curve — Christ, it was almost impossible to see now! — and a side road right that was little more than a cow path back into what appeared to be a shallow box canyon, part of it fenced, choked with willows or some similar tree. As he roared past, Davis looked for dust in the air down there, but didn't see any. He wondered if it was too dark to see it if it were there. He had no time for speculation. Every ounce of his energy was funneled into the job of driving.

The roadway became narrower still and the canyon walls closed in on both sides, the stream much narrowed, marked by water rushing through a narrow rock ravine with such speed that its whitewater looked silvery even in this terrible light. No turnoffs here, Davis thought. The Buick had to be still ahead.

Up ahead he caught a momentary flash of pinkish red light—the Buick, surely. He could get closer than this. He eased the Taurus a bit faster, feeling the back end slip and slide in minute losses of rear wheel bite. He didn't have time to glance at the instruments again, and maybe now he couldn't have read them in the gloom anyway.

The river canyon suddenly began to widen, and Davis drove out onto a broad meadow area, the stream off to the left somewhere behind a grove of aspen, a fenceline along the right to protect perhaps as much as sixty acres of what looked like cultivated field of some kind. The mountains seemed to have receded all around, were off in the dark where he couldn't pick them up now.

Ahead he saw the lights of the other vehicle flare for braking. He could not allow for much time if the bald man stopped; he might be stopping only to finish Brad off and dump his body in the ditch. Davis maintained speed.

The other car did stop, pulling off to the side of the road. Davis didn't know what the hell to do now, but he knew it wasn't a good time to count eenie meenies. Flicking on his headlights, he tipped the high-beam switch and started braking hard as the lights came fully onto the Buick on the roadside less than a hundred yards ahead.

Only it wasn't the Buick.

It was a dark-colored Japanese 4×4 pickup, and a youthful man and pretty girl with flaxen hair had just clambered out onto the roadway, fishing poles in hand. They looked up and froze with alarm as Davis skidded the Ford to a halt on the shoulder behind their truck, fixing them with his brights.

Rolling his window down, he yelled at them, "Did you see a Buick sedan on this road somewhere?"

"You'd better be careful!" the boy replied hoarsely. "I've got a gun in the truck!"

"Goddam it, did you see a dark-colored Buick back up the road?"

It was the girl who answered. "Yes, but we passed him when he turned off at Box Canyon."

"Shit!" Davis cranked the steering wheel hard left, pulled partway across the narrow roadway, backed around, and spun the wheel left a second time. The racket of his tires in the dirt and gravel was far worse than what the bald man had made back in town. The Taurus held a straight line, however, and pressed Davis lightly back in the seat as it accelerated.

Within ten or fifteen seconds he was going so fast that the car felt decidedly light on its springs, almost a projectile out of control. Davis did not ease off. He had screwed up. Maybe he had lost the trail altogether. Caution was the last thing he could afford now.

The situation portrayed here is roughly as follows: The viewpoint character in the chapter, Collie Davis, a close friend of hero Brad Smith, has just seen an unconscious Brad in a car speeding away from a motel in the small Colorado mountain town of Lake City. Davis recognizes the driver as a man intent on killing Brad, so Davis must pursue and try to prevent it.

The setting problem: Show rapid character movement during a car chase; remain focused on the desperate, high-speed action of the chase; yet keep the reader physically oriented to the movement through the setting, as well as to the car being pursued and the micro-environment inside Davis's vehicle.

Consider some details in the excerpt:

In the first paragraph, words like "running" and "grabbed" establish the high-speed, hectic quality of the action to follow. The direction, south, is established, along with the make of the other car and the existence of foothills in that direction. The last sentence sets Davis's car in motion for pursuit.

In the second paragraph, Davis gets the briefest glance at bystanders, a necessary detail to prevent the setting from being abstract at this point. Then the sound of the transmission is added for realistic impact on another of the reader's senses. (While most of this sequence stresses sight perceptions, you may notice a continuing attempt to mention other senses such as hearing whenever it seems appropriate.)

The fourth paragraph, beginning "Ahead . . . ," establishes spatial dimension, in this case the distance between the cars. The mention of red tail-lights and gravel gives the reader further concrete physical details — to put him into this setting.

The next paragraph, beginning "The gravel road. . . ," compresses a few moments, but gives additional details ("a series of curves" and "deep canyon") to keep the reader oriented. Dimness and the powdery dust thrown by the other car are again very specific physical orientation markers.

The sixth paragraph, beginning "Sweat stung," moves description of the setting almost inside Davis's brain, focusing on minutiae of the setting in such a way that a transition is then possible all the way out of the physical environment for a moment and inside Davis's thoughts. The remainder of this paragraph and the ones immediately following it are for reader contact with character emotion and thought process.

Later, an attempt is made to get the reader back into closer touch with the broader setting. "Sheer red rock walls" and the "hundred-foot rock face" plunge him, we hope, into physical awareness of the deepening canyon and the worsening condition of its "narrow and washboarded" road. In the next paragraph, the near-collision with a Jeep coming from the opposite direction is designed to put the reader more intensely in contact with the speed and dangerous lack of control involved in the setting. When Davis's car brushes the rock wall, we again become aware of sound.

In the paragraph starting with "Another curve," the reader, does not know it at the time because the viewpoint character doesn't know it, but the small canyon is where the pursued car actually turned off. It is important to orient the reader to this bit of the setting so that a return to it later will not come as a total surprise, but at the same time the view must be fleeting. Note that the viewpoint character looks for dust, does not see any, but wonders if it's too dark to see it even if it were there. Also notice a later sentence — "He had no time for speculation." You will find that inserting such statements into fast-moving descriptions of setting will help greatly in keeping the details brief and vivid; if the viewpoint character has no time to notice details, you can't be tempted to put them into your copy, and the reader is more likely to accept the ongoing rush of brief glimpses and impressions.

A few paragraphs later Davis moves out of the tight canyon setting and into different terrain with details such as "broad meadow area," "sixty acres," and "cultivated field." When he sees lights ahead, he reacts in action, rather than with any fine description, his response to the stimulus being the important thing.

The setting detail of the 4 × 4 vehicle and the two passengers changes the dramatic situation in a startling way. Details are brief, but the "dark-colored" pickup, "youthful man" and "pretty girl with flaxen hair" give enough evocative detail that the reader can imaginatively fill in the picture.

The remainder of the excerpt deals almost exclusively with a plot twist, returning Davis's, and the reader's, mind to the small box canyon mentioned so briefly but importantly at an earlier stage of the action. As Davis gets back into new violent action, the desperation of his inner setting — his mood — is shown by the startling expletive. The "racket of his tires in the dirt" is a concrete appeal to hearing, and is compared with the sound Davis heard earlier (prior to the portion quoted here) when the abductor's departure first alerted him to the situation. Davis's mood of intense worry and haste is emphasized again for several reasons: to motivate continuation of the chase at dangerous high speed (plot); to continue to characterize Davis's internal feelings (characterization), and to keep the reader mentally prepared for brief, fragmentary description as rapid movement through the story environment resumes (setting). This, it seems to me, is an excellent example of how setting can seldom be considered in isolation from other elements of storytelling; it relates to all of them, and they relate to it.

Although it is not readily apparent in this excerpt, the brief descriptions here set up reader orientation for much of what is to follow. The reader knows the next action will probably be in that box canyon glimpsed earlier; he knows the area is remote, that it is mountain country, that there are few people around, and that darkness has fallen. Thus one part of your story's description of setting can set up reader orientation for what is to follow in a subsequent section.

As a suggestion for further detailed study: You may wish to go back through this excerpt and study the language. For example, you might underline the strong action verbs in red and the sharply specific noun phrases (such as "hundred-foot rock face" and "crunching sound") in green. Count the number of words in many sentences and compute an average sentence length for my description of high-speed movement through setting. Can you draw any conclusions which might help you in your own work?

CONCLUSIONS

If you began this study of setting with the idea that it's a static physical backdrop for your story, this chapter more than any other so far should have opened your eyes. Setting is a dynamic aspect of storytelling. Movement can drastically alter your method of dealing with the setting. How you handle the setting can have a direct effect on your reader's story involvement and sense of plot pace. Setting is not a piece of canvas stuck on the back wall of your story; it is a moving, changing, exciting part of your total story fabric.

Most of the time, when you are showing a quick change of setting or rapid movement through a setting, you will be in a character's viewpoint. It may sound paradoxical when I say it, but the quality of your handling of setting at such times may be as dependent upon what you don't tell as on what you do. You must always remember how limited and fragmentary a viewpoint character's awareness may be . . . how overwhelming may be the sense of haste or confusion . . . how strong may be a few broad-brush impressions which can block out character awareness of any fine detail. Your ability to use highly selective detail may "make or break" your story sequences in which movement is part of the experience.

CHAPTER 13

THE STORY BEHIND YOUR SETTING

AT THE OPENING OF CHAPTER ONE, we defined setting as including historical background and cultural attitudes of a given place and time. Implicit in much of the discussion throughout later chapters has been the assumption that setting can indeed affect characters and their behavior. And we have mentioned history briefly, as well as mood and tone. In this chapter, however, we will look more specifically at the history of a setting and how such history might develop certain prevailing attitudes and feelings in its people, aspects you need to understand if your total story setting is to be convincing.

Now, you might assume that if your story setting is a totally imagined town and local area, knowledge of any real history or cultural attitudes is irrelevant. Nothing could be further from the truth. Except in science fiction, where you may be creating a wholly alien setting, your stories will be set in an identifiable region — the South, say, or eastern seaboard metroplex. So even if your particular town doesn't exist, it has to be convincing to the reader. And it can't be convincing if its history and cultural attitudes are totally at odds with what the reader knows and expects about the actual region.

STORY BACKGROUND

In an earlier chapter I told you about a tour of Oklahoma I did once, and the differences I found between people in the hills and on the plains. That's one example of how regional setting affects attitude. Here's another aspect of the same idea: Can you imagine taking the history and resulting cultural attitudes of a small midwestern town in the United States and trying to create a setting in South America based on the same kind of background and value system? The history of a place, and the outlook that history has created, is as vital and unique a part of story setting as any other factor — and it has to be right.

Your story setting in terms of past time — and the likely general attitudes and feelings the past will engender in its people — has to be correct if your story is to convince the reader. Even if you're writing a science fiction tale of an alien universe, you'll have to know the prevailing attitudes there, and you'll have to invent a history that would credibly create those attitudes. More often than not, however, you'll be dealing with an imaginary place in a very real region of the world, and your imagined microcosm has to be in harmony with the realities of that region.

The importance of history and regional attitude was forcibly brought home to me years ago when I moved from my native Ohio to central Oklahoma. I knew little of Oklahoma history, either long- or short-term, and had a devil of a time understanding how most of the people seemed to feel and think about some things. Only when I began to understand the history of the region could I see where some of the puzzling comments and behavior came from.

Here is what I started out knowing, or *thinking* I knew: Oklahoma was a western state, probably with a lot of cowboys in it. There were Indians there, and oil production. I thought it was prosperous and optimistic, with at least traces of a frontier adventuresomeness.

What I found in general was somewhat different. One of the first things that struck me was racism; there were still segregated lunch counters and restricted sections on public buses, and in the county courthouse I was shocked to find a restroom marked "White Men Only." Jokes based on racial stereotyping were all too common. I didn't see many cowboys, and the Indians I saw were generally acculturated into the lower economic strata of white society, and the victims of a racial bias quieter but even more pervasive than that afflicting blacks. The small towns seemed broken-down and poor, and large sections of the larger cities looked bright and shiny, as if they had been built yesterday. Most surprising of all, perhaps, most of the white people I met in all walks of life seemed angrily defensive about being Oklahomans, and went to great lengths to protest that they were *not* "Okies." The state seemed to have a galloping inferiority complex, and an anger to go with it.

As I listened to the people, thought about my experiences and studied the history a bit, many of these surprising attitudes were explained.

Oklahoma only became a state in 1907, less than half a century before I first moved there. It had seen a continual cycle of booms and busts in the oil business, and was at that time in something of a bust. The small towns looked run-down because I was seeing the original housing in many instances, cheap pioneer construction now falling down after a life-span of almost fifty years and not being replaced because times were presently hard. In the more prosperous cities, some of the buildings that looked like they had been built yesterday *had* been built yesterday; the cities were in the process of rejuvenating themselves after the initial cycle of poor construction and subsequent decay.

As to the social attitudes, nothing was forgiven but a great deal was explained when I began to learn that Oklahoma's land runs were made primarily by poor *southern* whites who had failed other places and went to the new territory for one last desperate try. (Similarly, I understood a later-detected narrow definition of moral acceptability—Oklahoma was still a dry state then, for example—when I read of the early influx of conservative fundamentalist religious groups and their stubborn adherence to their traditional strict, unyielding view of what constituted acceptable behavior.)

A certain air of lawlessness puzzled me at first, and then began to make sense in a way when I saw how decades of prohibition had created a society with laws against liquor—and a flourishing bootlegger business which circumvented the law.

The state's seeming inferiority complex was hardest to understand. Despite everything negative I have mentioned, Oklahoma had a dynamism about it, and clean air, and great freedom and opportunity. Why, then, did everyone seem so angrily defensive?

I learned that John Steinbeck's novel *The Grapes of Wrath* had infuriated and insulted Oklahoma people. I had read the novel as a collegian in Ohio, and thought the Okies portrayed were splendid, brave, noble people, the impression I feel sure Steinbeck intended. But in Oklahoma people were already hurt and oversensitive to imagined slights because of insults from Californians who had not welcomed a flood of homeless "Sooners" who went to that state during the Dust Bowl days. The result was that Oklahomans felt Steinbeck's novel made them all look stupid, dirty, poor and worthless, and they bitterly resented it. This was why they were so defensive and argumentative.

Thus a growing understanding of Oklahoma's history—its land runs, the primary regional background of its people, its youth, its oil booms and busts, and its disastrous part in the Dust Bowl and in Steinbeck's novel—helped me understand prevailing attitudes which otherwise made little sense.

I've told this rather extended personal story merely to make a point: A people will be influenced by their past; a people's general attitudes and moods will influence the world of your story—will be a vital aspect of the setting. If you want a totally convincing setting, you must include history and the feelings and attitudes which come from it.

This does not necessarily mean that you will dump huge blocks of history into your story, or inflict on your reader sociological explanations of character attitudes or behavior. It does mean, however, that some brief explanations may be salted into omniscient passages or casual observations by characters. Such brief comments linking history and attitude will add great verisimilitude to the setting.

GETTING INFORMATION

The best way to get the feel and history of a region, of course, is to visit it and stay long enough to get past whatever tourist veneer may disguise the cultural reality. This may mean an extended stay, or several short ones. If you can afford such an expedition or expeditions, you will be richly rewarded with continuing discoveries that will give your resulting story a vitality and depth it otherwise could not have.

But what if you don't have the time or money to spend days or weeks in your desired regional setting? Then you are reduced to studying books, maps, brochures and possibly video or film about the region.

This is not as much fun, but it's a possible alternative.

There are many "remote" sources available for learning about a region's history and attitudes. As you begin your inquiry into an area, you will likely develop specialized sources of information in a short time. Appendix 1 makes a number of suggestions on developing such sources. You might want to read the few general comments that follow here, then turn to that appendix for a fuller discussion.

Here are some of the possible sources you may check for information about your setting:

1. Your public library. A regional or area history will almost surely be available off the shelf or via interlibrary loan. Consult your librarian if a search of the card file or computer database doesn't suggest a few titles. Remember that most states require a grade school or high school course in local history; such textbooks should be available, and often include the kind of general information you seek. Also, social and cultural historians began contributing valuable state studies during the 1930s, when government projects funded them, and such work continues today. Many states also are the subject of a "roadside history" book, designed so motorists can visit historic sites on the highways, and state or local magazines and special periodicals may be a gold mine of information.

2. Your college library. If you can gain access to a college library, further resources are available to you. More specialized histories of towns, religious groups, etc., may be found here. Don't overlook master's degree theses and doctoral dissertations in such areas as history, sociology, economics and social work.

3. Your state or area historical society. Although these spe-

cialize in your own area, you may be surprised to learn what resources are available through interlibrary loan, on microfilm or microfiche, or on computer disk. Genealogical collections often reside in state libraries of this type, too, and could include basic genealogical references for other areas of the country. Such materials may provide valuable insights into long-standing attitudes and values of a region.

4. Government documents. The United States has studied and analyzed virtually every aspect of life in this country, from agricultural history and practices to sexual behavior and consumer spending. Most cities of moderate size or larger have a telephone number listed for assistance to citizens. You can order documents this way, or procure a guide to many documents available by mail order from Washington.

5. Your local bookstore. Most will have a variety of magazines. There probably will also be a "travel" section, and browsing here may uncover a specific guidebook or history you will find relevant. Be sure to consult the bibliographies in the back of such books for leads to other source publications on the subject.

6. Correspondence. Even small towns these days have Chambers of Commerce and/or tourist bureaus. Don't hesitate to write for historical or cultural information. These offices exist to answer such queries, and some material you may receive free of charge. States have tourist bureaus, too, and industrial development offices designed to provide demographic, attitudinal and all sorts of other information for potential tourists, PR firms or businesses considering relocation. This material may answer many questions for you.

7. Computer sources. If you have a CD-ROM drive, you may already have a source of historical information on compact disk. Whole encyclopedias are available, and many regional histories. There are several fine commercial products for sale on floppy disks, including some which show historic trends, industrial production, religious groupings, financial standings, and many other aspects of an area's attitudinal life. To find out where to obtain any of these materials for your computer, browse through any of the top monthly computer magazines for a wealth of ads for them.

8. Interviews. Don't forget to ask about them among your friends and associates. You may often find that a friend has a

friend who was raised in the area you're interested in. If you get lucky this way, by all means seek out an interview. People usually love to talk about places in their past, and you will get not only information but a real insight into the attitudes of the person you are interviewing; such attitudes may be typical of the region.

USING THE INFORMATION

Having consulted some or all of these possible sources, you'll be ready to take the same steps another writer would take after visiting an area to study its history and attitudes. Essentially, you will ask yourself:

- What in the history of this place is uniquely formative of prevailaing attitudes and feelings?
- What are these prevailing attitudes and feelings?
- How can I present the characteristic area attitudes and their background cause in my story?
- What part does this aspect of setting play in the working out of my story?

If you have done your homework and then honestly decide that there's nothing especially significant in the historical background or regional attitudes of the people as far as your particular story is concerned, well and good. Your effort still will not have been wasted because you can proceed confidently, knowing you aren't likely to make any factual errors such as having a Dallas cabdriver view the world the way one in New York might, or having upstanding citizens openly frequent a roadside bar in a small town in the heart of Southern Baptist country. And more likely you won't just prevent such obvious setting errors. You will also get a keener feel for your entire story world because you will know where the story people have come from — what makes them and their peers "tick."

That's why history and attitude are such an important part of your story setting. Getting them right will not only prevent mistakes damaging to credibility, it will also help you better plan the events likely to motivate your characters ... stir them up ... make them feel passion. Your story will be made more believable at the same time it is drawing additional feeling and even fervor from the historical background and prevailing sentiments of the place.

As an exercise, pause here and consider—on paper—your own area, the place where you live now. Briefly write down what you believe the general feeling of the place is in terms of how people feel about themselves, their setting and their lives, and what they believe in and care about. Then try to find and write down some of the historical background for the area that tended to make people the way they are. Can you identify the attitudes? Can you define any of them as special to your area? Can you find the historical or perhaps sociological reason for them?

Such practice on an area that you know well should help you prepare for checking out an area that's relatively unfamiliar to you.

If you haven't done so earlier, this would be a fine time to consult Appendices 1 and 2. These go into further detail and other aspects of researching a setting and may provide you with additional ideas for investigation of how a place was, and how the past influences the present.

CHAPTER 14

SETTING AND STYLE

A THOROUGHLY DETAILED STUDY of writing techniques in presentation of story setting is well beyond the scope of this book. But questions often asked—and errors frequently seen in student manuscripts—suggest that a few observations and bits of advice would not be out of order.

Your style as a fiction writer may have already developed over time, or may just be in the process of developing. In either case, it is likely that you will write best if you force yourself never to try to be "fancy" or "inspiring" or anything of that kind in developing your writing style. The best style usually is no visible style at all—prose that is crisp, clean, clear and transparent: a pane of glass through which your reader experiences the story directly, without ever being aware of the words. Far too much "stylish" writing is really affected writing, and while there may be a few readers out there who would appreciate such stuff, the fact is that your story has been lost the first moment a reader starts noticing your style rather than following the story's events.

The bottom line: In handling setting, as in all other parts of your fiction writing, strive for directness and simplicity. Such writing is the most graceful and effective of all.

SOME TRUTHS

It is also a fact that handling setting often involves description of some kind, and it is in description that writers most often fall prey to the temptation to write "pretty" or "poetic" passages. Therefore, it's vital in talking about setting to begin any discussion of verbal technique with truths which have been stated before, and will always be true:

- Write simply and directly, and don't get fancy.
- Never use a big word when a small one will do.
- Write short sentences. Write short paragraphs.
- Never strain for an effect, and never try to be poetic.
- Remember that clarity is your bedrock stylistic goal.

These rules might all be summarized briefly: When in doubt, take it out. If you are not absolutely certain that a turn of phrase is accomplishing the desired effect—and the story can go on without it—then don't put the phrasing in at all, or if it's in your draft, delete it on rewrite. Few things will disgust a busy editor—or more quickly brand you an amateur—than overwriting.

You know what that is: a seemingly endless round-and-round the verbal rosebush, trying to pile more and more adjectives on something in the setting so it will be "clearer." Or tacking a batch of weak adverbs onto a verb that was wobbly to begin with, in an attempt to make the verb more forceful.

Here is an example:

A warmly cheerful and welcoming fire was burning brightly inside the large, dark, sinister cavern, while slow-moving shadows could be discerned on the high, pale walls of rock.

What's wrong with this? Just about everything! Consider: The writer wants to show the setting in a vivid way, but the approach is all wrong. Instead of seeking out strong basic words, the writer stuck on all sorts of qualifying adjectives and adverbs ("warmly cheerful," "welcoming," "large, dark, sinister," etc.) instead of trying to be simple and direct. You may come up with a better rewrite, but here is one possibility:

A campfire blazed inside the great cave. Shadows danced on the high rock walls.

You may quarrel with use of the verb "blazed," and wish to substitute something like "burned brightly." You may argue, too, that "great cave" is not sufficiently evocative. Is "danced" a cliché? Perhaps you can come up with better wording.

Regardless of such quibbles, I think you will agree that the second effort is improved by slashing some of the weak adjectives and adverbs and attempting to find stronger nouns and verbs that don't require such crutches. A good, specific noun will seldom need many adjectives to modify it. A strong action verb will seldom require the help of an adverb. Therefore, it's obvious that you can, as one editor advised me, "look for adjectives and adverbs, and kill them!" or you can possibly avoid the temptation to use them in the first place by seeking out strong specific nouns and strong action verbs.

A further observation about these examples may be in order. You may have noticed that in the original a fire "was burning," while in the suggested revision a "fire blazed." If we had chosen to substitute "burned" for "blazed," the basic meaning would have been the same, but for better style: Always use the simple past tense if you can in describing things. Thus you will not write, "Rain was falling . . . ," but instead will teach yourself to write, "Rain fell. . . . " You will not write, "Evening was nearing . . . ," but instead, "Evening neared. . . . " (or perhaps better: "Darkness neared," darkness being more specific than evening).

Also, avoid the passive voice. You will *not* say things like, "The night was made worse when the rain began . . . ," but instead will say something closer to "The night worsened when the rain began." The use of compound verb forms and weak passives in description is often tempting, but almost always bad. Compound verb forms are not the most direct way to get the job done, and passives are weak; description always walks on the dangerous edge of being too slow and dramatically weak anyway, so don't make the risk greater than it already is.

When this was first pointed out to me years ago, I protested (briefly) that it's not quite the same thing to say "a fire burned" and "a fire was burning." Being a refugee from an English department, I argued that "fire burned" implied that the fire had burned in the past and was now over, while "fire was burning" connoted that it was still burning in the story present. "Pick nits all you want," my writing coach replied. "Try it my way and you'll never go back." He was right. Once I habitually used the simple past tense, all my descriptions of setting seemed magically more vibrant.

Look for weak verb forms, pallid nouns, crutch adjectives and limping adverbs in your own copy. If you find them, fix them!

THE PURPLE PATCH

Another aspect of straightforward descriptive writing style is the ability to avoid poetic flights of fancy and unnecessary big words. You have perhaps encountered such a flight in someone else's copy—surely not your own!—and know why composition teachers call such an effusion a "purple patch."

Here's an example of a purple patch:

> Rising, chanting, ever-changing, in a never-ending cacophony of ululation, the zephyr-breath of the mighty planet's ceaseless, restless celestial motion, driven alike by the massive depth of ocean and rising of a miniscule breeze from the golden, petal-like wings of a gossamer butterfly, pressed insistent lips against the diaphanous opacity of the chill pane.

Wow. Gorgeous, huh?—until you stop and figure out what the writer was trying to say, which was: Cold wind blew against the frosty window.

It's been said before, but the point is worth making again. Such outrages against writing style most often occur when the writer has "stopped to describe." Therefore, one good way to avoid the temptation to write purple patches is to seldom stop your storytelling to describe. If you are intent on keeping your setting descriptions brief and maintaining focus on the characters and the plot inside the setting, then few chances to write a purple patch will arise.

Instead of burying yourself, your story and your reader under a trash-pile of verbiage, look for the *feel* of a place or time, and then seek out concrete details to evoke that feeling. As mentioned in chapter eleven and elsewhere, the feeling might be one of joyfulness or isolation or loneliness. Identify it, then ask yourself what specific concrete details will evoke the feeling in as few words as possible. You can count on your reader to fill in the details if you give him precisely the right clues on which to build.

That's why, for example, I risked using the word "blazed" in an example earlier in this chapter, and why I contented myself with calling the site a "great cave." I am not sure precisely what the word "blazed" will conjure in the reader's mind, but I feel sure it will have something to do with bright, leaping flames, great heat and vigor. Exactly what picture "blazed" will give the reader beyond that, I don't know. But I don't care; his own imagining will be better for him than any further avalanche of details I might try to foist upon him. Similarly, I count on "great cave" evoking in his mind his own mind-picture of the feeling of greatness and cave-ness. Will it be Carlsbad, or an earthen hole he played in as a child? I don't care; I would rather he work from my feeling-evoking words, and draw his own feeling-packed mind-picture, than try to study through some laborious description of mine.

Readers love to draw setting pictures in their own imagination. They will, provided you give them the right feel for the place, and the few precise words designed to evoke that feeling.

How do you find those few precise words? You do so by seeking out specific, concrete details in the setting which will produce the desired evocation. As an example, suppose you first laboriously wrote something unacceptable like the following:

It was a cold and bitter night. Phillip felt chilled, and when the sleet began, he felt colder. Dark clouds rolled in. The mercury fell. Icy wind began to blow. Walking home alone, Phillip was buffeted by the wind.

This is not too bad. Short words, short sentences, little strained "poetry." But it lacks feeling-focus. What are we trying to evoke here? Cold? Wind? Loneliness? Darkness? A short segment like this can't evoke everything at once, and maybe the story situation dictates brevity, as it often does.

But perhaps we can improve things. Let's decide that what we want to evoke in the reader concerning this bit of setting is a feeling of *chill and loneliness*. Having decided this, we can have a stab at revision something like this:

> Alone, Phillip trudged home. Violent wind battered him, driving pinprick sleet into his face.

Possibly this brief segment will get the job done for us. Suppose, on the other hand, we wish to use the same general setting details to evoke a different mood in the reader, one of *longing for home*. In such a case we might produce a segment like this:

> Hurrying against the strong wind, Phillip squinted through the darkness for the first sight of his cabin window. It would be good to get home to the warmth of his stove and the stout protection of the cabin's log walls.

In both of the above examples, notice that indentification of desired feeling provides the framework inside which a brief and focused description can be written.

ADDING CONTRAST

Another helpful gambit you can use in seeking brevity and evocative accuracy is the use of contrast. On its simplest level, what we are talking about here is how a dark cloud will look darker against an otherwise bright sky, or how much more dreary an old building will look if you stand it beside a fine, fresh new one for the sake of the contrast. It always helps the vividness and evocativeness of your writing if you can pinpoint a sharp contrast: barren black tree branches seen against a snow-colored wintry sky, for example, or a scream piercing the total silence of a summer afternoon in the country, or the glitter of diamonds on a black velvet cloth.

The trick here is to identify the object you wish to emphasize, figure out what specific sensuous characteristic of that object should be stressed, and then find the right object to stand it beside, or background to display it against, for the maximum contrast.

In sight contrasts, look for dark against light, smooth against rough, color against pallor, smallness against vastness, or brightness against dullness. In sound contrasts, look for loudness against silence, pleasing sound against discordance, harshness against smoothness. Ask yourself: "What specific aspect of the setting do I want to make vivid?" Then: "What can I place beside it to make it stand out even more?"

Suppose you want to show how loudly that truck is idling at the corner traffic light? First make sure no other cars are on the street when you show it, and make the scene a lazy afternoon or evening, very, very quiet otherwise. Then the truck's idling will be not only loud, but deafening. Or perhaps you would like to emphasize how small a house is, and how isolated; take it out of that tight little woods and stand it alone on a vast and windy hilltop, surrounded by a thousand acres of empty prairie. (Does this mean, incidentally, that you will sometimes tinker with minor aspects of your setting simply to make things more vivid? Of course.)

LEARNING TO OBSERVE

First-hand observation will help you clarify some of these stylistic techniques for yourself once you are aware of them. I encourage you to look at parts of the real setting-world around you, and think about how you would portray them. Look at the tree in your yard or nearby park — *really* look at it, for a change. How could you place that in your story setting and make it real and vibrant for your reader? Really look at that city bus as it approaches your stop. How could you put that bus into your story and make it practically leap off the page for your reader, so that it becomes a tremendously vital and real part of the setting?

Make notes as you hone your observation-description skills, write practice paragraphs. Make sure they're not long, static paragraphs, but brief, evocative ones, centered on a mood. If you don't like a description you've produced, go back and rewrite it using stronger verbs and more specific nouns, or using a different feeling as the focus point, or putting something different into the setting for useful contrast.

Such accurate observation, creative thought and careful verbal revision will soon result in surer and more skillful use of all the other techniques we have covered in this book. In handling setting, the use of precise language is mandatory, because your words are the conveyance of everything you know and your reader needs to know. Nothing else will work unless your verbal arsenal is on target.

So important is verbal technique in setting, as a matter of fact, that we cannot leave the subject with the discussion given in this chapter. In chapter fifteen we will pursue the subject a bit more, with a number of highly specific exercises and work suggestions.

CHAPTER 15

EXERCISES TO SHARPEN YOUR SETTINGS

BE WARNED IN ADVANCE: This chapter is designed to make you practice some of the things you've learned in earlier chapters. None of it will be especially difficult for you now, but doing the suggested exercises correctly will require some investment of time as well as effort—and there's even a requirement for that aspect of fiction-writing which all amateurs dread and all selling professionals do: rewriting.

FACTUAL DATA IN A SETTING

Let's suppose you have the following information in your notebook after visiting a small town and making observations and then doing other factual research at the library.

> The name of the town is Elk City, and it's in the western part of Montana. In a valley in the Sapphire Mountains. Population is 3,000. County Seat of Morgan County. Courthouse on town square downtown, old brick building, two stories, with a dome. City hall, a small stucco structure, is nearby on Main Street. The town is quiet, but sometimes trucks going by on the nearby highway make a big racket. A bell in the tower at the First Presbyterian Church tolls the hour. Elk City has a city manager and city commission, five commissioners elected at large. Small police department and fire department, antiquated equipment. Sheriff's

department in the basement of the courthouse is old and grungy. Sheriff has four deputies. It's cold in Elk City in the winters, cool in the summers. The surrounding mountains are tall, jagged and beautiful. No other town of any size nearby — people drive ninety miles to Missoula for major shopping expeditions. It's an easygoing place with a population on the elderly side, and hunters and fishermen visit a lot. Nothing much ever seems to happen. Some of the side streets are dirt only, and in the summers they're dusty. An old, open-pit copper quarry nearby, now abandoned, has water in it which sometimes smells bad on the hottest summer days. During the long, snowy winters, of course, this is no problem. It was a pleasant summer day, seventy degrees, when you visited last July 7 and 8.

Elk City was founded by a man named John Jergens in the 1880s. He found a small vein of silver nearby, and for a few years the town boomed with silver mining. When the silver played out in the 1890s, copper was discovered and the big quarry, now an abandoned pit, provided steady work and income for about a hundred families. As copper production decreased, the town declined steadily, and by the 1920s it was about the size it is today. Old-timers still yearn for the good old days. Every year they have a Frontier Days celebration on September 1. Parade, community picnic, band performance in old Jergens City Park. People are proud of sticking it out in Elk City, and think one day the town will come back. They've been saying that for more than fifty years now.

The town's five churches provide the center of social activity. There's also a Moose Lodge. People often gather for coffee at the Chicken Shack Cafe on Main Street or the Big Sky Motel's coffee shop on the edge of town, on Highway 16. The local paper, a weekly, is called *The Bugle*.

Elk City used to be on a railroad passenger line, but that's long since closed. The old rock station is falling down. Once a day, about 4 P.M., a Montana Rail Link freight train pulls through on its way north, not stopping. The diesel engine usually blows its whistle at the Main Street crossing and farther north, at Bryson Road. The train comes back through, headed south, about midnight, and blows its horn again. It's a mournful sound at night.

Movie theater, the Ritz is closed permanently and boarded up. Major street names other than Main, which runs east-west: High Street, Bluff Street, Sapphire Ave., Higgins Street, Selby Ave. The grade and high schools are on Selby. Sometimes in the winter, deer and even elk wander down out of the aspens and lodgepole pines on the mountainsides and walk right down Main Street. There are black bear nearby, too, and sometimes a mountain lion is reported. Area ranchers and sheepmen are bitter about federal and state laws protecting wolves and the occasional mountain lion.

Study the above information, then duplicate Nancy Berland's Setting Research Form (Appendix 2), and fill in a copy of the form from the facts given.

After doing this work, think about the kind of characters and plots that might be used in this general setting. For example, you might write about members of the local political scene, suddenly thrust into a crisis when it is discovered that pollution from the old copper mine has poisoned all local sources of water. Or you might put a romance in this setting, with the conflict stemming from the fact that the heroine is a native who loves the place, and her lover is a visitor intent on buying up property and changing everything by turning it into a gaudy gambling oasis.

Think a bit, too, about some of the stories that might not work well, or at all, in this setting: a grim, police-method murder investigation might never work because the town's law enforcement is small and primitive; a plot involving members of a large juvenile gang would probably be out of the question because the town does not have large numbers of juveniles on the loose, and no stated crime problem. (I suggest that you think of these "impossibles" briefly just to further clarify your understanding of how setting enables — or precludes — certain kinds of stories.)

Having done all this work, take another step. Select the bare bones of a plot and a cast of your own that you believe might work in this setting. Then, on another sheet of paper or two, make a preliminary list of other general aspects of the setting which you believe you would have to learn about if you were actually going to write this imagined book. This list might include "ethnic makeup of population," "voting record in general elections," or even something like "worst drouth in area history." This will be *your* list, growing out of your ideas about what your story plot should be in the given setting.

Having done this, if you can hone your list into one or more specific questions—about anything at all that you think you might need to know—be sure to do so, making them as detailed and lengthy as possible. Then ponder a bit where you might get all this additional information if you were really getting ready to write the book.

Finally, write a 300-word description of the setting as you would use it in terms of mood and viewpoint. If you were planning a romance, for example, your selection of sensory details might be generally sunny, summery, ruggedly inviting. And your selection of factual material would tend to emphasize the positive and upbeat. If you were planning a gothic terror story, on the other hand, you would be shooting for quite a different tone, and your selected details probably would tend more toward the dark, the isolated and the bizarre.

If you worked conscientiously on this assignment, you went through the essential process for checking out, analyzing, and using information in order to present a credible and effective story setting. In addition, although no stress was placed on the fact at the time, you also produced a lengthy piece of writing about setting.

Going through the process in this way is its own reward; nothing teaches better than practice. To assist you further, however, here is a suggested list of questions which might help you analyze how well you did on the job.

- What viewpoint did you select to describe this setting? Why?
- What mood did you select? Does the mood grow directly out of your perception of the given facts about the setting,

from your idea about a plot problem to put in that setting, from your conception of the kind of character you would use as the viewpoint in such a setting, or on some other factor?

- Did you find or imaginatively add some salient setting aspect which might recur in your story as a central point of focus or symbol? What is it? Why did you choose it?
- What single, dominant impression about this setting did you identify as a centralizing point for your treatment of it?
- Did you identify anything in the history of the setting which would contribute to a prevailing cultural attitude which might be useful in your story?
- What kind of central character would work best for you in this setting?
- Did you introduce that character in your 300 words? If not, should you have done so?
- Was your description of setting static, a "stop-action" picture, or was there movement of some kind? Does consideration of this question suggest possible revision to you?
- Could this setting unify an otherwise fragmentary plot? How?
- Could this setting possibly become virtually a character itself?
- What contrasts if any did you use in describing this setting?
- Did you avoid weak passives in your writing?
- Did you use strong action verbs and specific nouns?
- Do you find a lot of adjectives and adverbs that ought to be "killed?"
- Do you habitually do this much work on setting for your stories?

In thinking back over previous chapters, you may come up with other self-check questions you want to ask. My list is, as stated, only suggestive. We learn our writing craft from trial and error, from failure, from praise, from teachers, from studying other writers, and from analyzing our own work in a critical (but not negative) manner. It's not enough to read about technique.

Practice — and thoughtful self-analysis — are mandatory if you are to grow in the craft.

For these reasons, it's never wise to rush through an assignment like the one above. Even if some of the work seems unnecessary, you never know where it might lead you. Work that may seem like drudgery at times may provide an insight that will vastly improve your fiction.

OBSERVATION IN THE FIELD

Find a local site that's outside your usual haunts. This may be a park you've never visited, a courtroom downtown, a cafe down the road somewhere, or a church or school you've noticed but never visited. Taking a notebook (and small recorder, if you have one), go to that unfamiliar place and spend at least an hour. Observe details. Make notes. Record sounds if possible. Try to identify the feel of the place. If there are people there, note how they look, how they dress, how they talk, their ages, their general demeanor, what they talk about, how they seem to feel, and what they are doing. Think about using this place in a setting.

Upon returning home — and within twenty-four hours while your memory is fresh — write a 300-word description of this site as if you planned to use it as the setting for a story.

After completing the setting description, use the questions listed for the first exercise to analyze this story setting.

Additionally, this exercise provides a good self-analysis of your writing style in handling setting material. Consider the following questions, and others like them:

• How many different senses are represented in your writing? (To facilitate analysis, you may wish to go through your copy and underline sight impressions in red, let's say, sounds in blue, odors in green, and so on.) Does one sense predominate? Did you overlook something that you might have usefully said about the setting if you had remembered another sense?
• How many adverbs and adjectives do you find? Can you kill any?

- Look for weak passive constructions. Repair them.
- Can you strengthen any verbs? Make any nouns more specific and concrete?
- Does your writing here evoke a specific feeling or mood in the reader? (Did you think about that while writing?)
- How many words of three or more syllables do you find? There shouldn't be many—big words usually hint at obscurity, and you want clarity.
- Write down what conclusions you can draw about your own writing tendencies at this point. For example, do you tend to use weak passives? Do you tend to adopt an omniscient viewpoint without thinking about it? Do you enrich your copy with multiple sense impressions, or do you tend to concentrate only on sight, for example?

Finally, rewrite the segment you prepared for this exercise. Improve it, knowing what you now see more clearly following your self-analysis.

LEARNING FROM A WRITER YOU LIKE

Seek to become a more consciously aware critic at the same time you read for pleasure or relaxation.

For this assignment, study a few pages of a story by a writer you admire. Find a section in the work which clearly deals with story setting. Mark up this copy—photocopy pages from the magazine or book, and work from the copies, if you can't bear to mark on the original.

Try to note, look for, question, and mark as many aspects as possible of this writer's handling of setting. Marginally annotate mood. Underline strong verbs.

Repeat the process outlined in the first two exercises. Again, try to write down some conclusions, even if the work seems only to verify things you knew before. Noting them again will deepen your understanding and retention of principles.

LEARNING FROM YOUR OWN COPY

Go back into your own story files and pull out a chapter or section dealing with setting. Go through the entire process of analysis outlined on earlier pages of this chapter.

Then, rigorously analyze any mistakes or slips you may have uncovered and ask yourself how you would handle this setting problem differently today. Are there gaps in your factual base? Does the setting lack feeling? Is the prose "purple" at times?

Rewrite the segment if you are now dissatisfied with it— even if it's part of something you previously sold. (The day you can't improve is the day you stop having a future as a writer.)

KNOWING YOUR OWN TENDENCIES

With regard to most of the work done for this chapter, you should seriously consider a fact mentioned fleetingly at an earlier point. That is: In going through the exercises, you may have exhibited previously unexamined creative tendencies of your own in dealing with setting. Having done this work and thought about it, you can perhaps see yourself more clearly. Did you let yourself get impatient? (I always do, and have to struggle against this known tendency in myself.) In the sample of your earlier work that you looked at, did you perhaps discover a previously unnoticed tendency toward purple prose or weak passive constructions in your writing style when describing setting? Did you discover that you always tend to adopt the same kind of story viewpoint in dealing with setting, and had never realized before that you did this?

Some of your ingrained creative tendencies are probably excellent. Others may be counterproductive or even destructive. Study yourself as well as others, and try to see your own work in a clearer, more objective light.

Such self-analysis of your tendencies as a writer not only

makes you more aware of what kind of writer you are at the moment, it may reveal to you new directions . . . new tasks to be undertaken . . . new possibilities for growth. In this way, the truth will truly set you free to become a far better writer than you ever imagined you might be.

CHAPTER 16

A PROGRAM FOR FURTHER STUDY AND GROWTH

IF WE HAVE ACCOMPLISHED anything in this study, I hope it has made you more aware of the importance of your fiction settings, and how setting interacts with so many other story factors. Setting, as you now see clearly, is far more than a painted physical backdrop behind the stage of your story's action; its effects ripple into all other aspects of your storytelling.

The observations and brief assignments included in this book were designed to increase both your awareness and technical agility in working with setting. You may already feel better qualified than ever before to handle setting problems. But work in this area, like most aspects of writing fiction, is never entirely done. All of us must continue to strive to sharpen our perceptions, our skills, and our ability to observe our own work as well as that of others.

Having finished this book, you are now just at the beginning of continuing work. How you proceed from this point will depend on many factors, including available time, the kind of fiction you want to write, and your discovered strengths and weaknesses. However you work to grow from this point forward, there are a few things you can do, and a few questions you can keep in mind, that will provide focus for the days ahead.

KEEPING TRACK

First and foremost, you need to develop a repository for your ongoing study of setting. You may already have one, in the form of a daily journal or one or more notebooks in which you make notations about the writing craft. Or perhaps you have a series of file folders where you collect notes, newspaper and magazine pieces or photos that might be useful one day in depicting a setting. If you have such a system for regularly making notes or keeping research material, I urge you to expand your use of it in ways to be mentioned shortly. If you do not have a journal or any kind of file for observations and general writing data, then consider starting one immediately.

I happen to have three such information repositories. One is a simple spiral-bound notebook of the kind students use. The second is a modest collection of file folders in a metal cabinet. The third is a small bookcase whose shelves are packed with maps, travel brochures, books, photographs and a few travel tapes (both audio and video), most of which I made myself.

In the notebook journal I regularly record information on my sales and royalties, as well as ideas for future projects and personal observations about possible characters, plots and settings. This is the place where I transfer short setting notes that I might have jotted down during a trip somewhere, for example.

I always carry some sort of smaller and easily portable notebook on trips, even short ones to places where I have been before. A company called Stationers, Inc., in Richmond, Virginia, makes a "Reporter's Note Book" that I favor; it's spiral-bound, with vertical flip-over, lined pages, and its dimensions are eight inches tall by four inches wide, a size that I can slip into an inside coat pocket, or a female writer might easily carry inside a normal-size purse. My setting notes might include a page or two of specific description or something as brief as a note made recently which read in full: "Ample late-summer rainfall makes aspens turn more red in the fall?" When I return from a trip somewhere, as already stated, I transfer these notes, often fragmentary, to the pages of the journal and discard the original notebook pages.

The same procedure serves well if you are making a more carefully planned trip to "scope out" an actual setting. In such cases, however, a still camera, a video camera if you have one, and a small cassette recorder will also come in handy. As discussed in Appendix 1, the recorder and camera may be invaluable during interviews. But also, you can sometimes gain great insight into the sounds of a place by simply recording several minutes of general background noise, then replaying it later.

Why is this so? While on the site and engrossed primarily in what you can see, you may overlook normal sounds that are vital to the setting, such things as the sound of traffic, a distant train, foghorns in the night, perhaps the barking of dogs. When you play back such a random audiotape later, you often hear things you missed at the time because you were distracted by something else entirely.

On any field trip, you should look for the local tourist information office or chamber of commerce, and see what brochures and maps may be free for the taking. These can go into one of your file folders or on a bookshelf.

When you know you have repositories for setting information, that very fact can motivate you to be more alert to gathering new data, whether you plan to use it immediately or not. If you are actively researching for a known project, you might use a variation of the Nancy Berland setting form found in Appendix 2. Having worked with a form like this a few times, however, you will find that asking some of its questions becomes second nature to you, but later transfer of data to a file copy of such a form puts information into a more-or-less standard format, making it easier to file, quicker to find later, and simpler to use even long after the observations have been made.

What form your own setting repository will take is up to you. These few observations are meant to stimulate you to come up with your own system. You may elect to use 5 × 7 file cards, or a directory on your computer's hard disk. Format is not as important as having a place, and feeding it information on a regular, sustained basis. The work will pay dividends for immediate projects and future ones that you haven't even imagined yet. It will also keep you focussed on aspects of setting vital to your stories.

Several chapters in this book have suggested aspects and uses of setting that should alert you to the kinds of information you should record. The Nancy Berland form is another fine guide. If at first you worry that you might forget crucial questions to ask when you are researching a setting, let me provide you with a short list to keep in mind as a starting point:

- What does this place feel like to you?
- What specific aspects of the setting make you feel that way?
- What do you know of the history of the place?
- What do you know about identifiable local attitudes?
- What is the dominant source of light here? How bright is it? What is its color? How does it contribute to the feeling of the place?
- What is the sense of space here? Vast? Cramped? Open? Closed?
- What three characteristic sounds can you identify?
- Is your sense of smell important in this setting?
- Is there a central landmark or possible setting symbol?
- What dramatic plot possiblities do you see here?
- What kind of character would you most likely put in this setting?
- How would you describe this place from an omniscient vantage point? From the viewpoint of a character?

Of course this is only a suggestive list, the kind I happen to carry around in my own mind. Your genre, interests and tendencies may lead to the development of different questions. The point is that any general list of questions helps focus your efforts in gathering new setting information, and having a general focus also helps you organize whatever filing system you choose to set up for such information.

CONCLUSION

Learning the value of setting is just the beginning of your quest for excellence in storytelling. As you hone your skills and develop your setting-presentation techniques, you will build a database and sharpen your powers of research and observation through field trips and careful recording of the things you find.

It's a lifelong process, learning to be more sensitive to the places and people around you, but it's a process that is not only rewarding in terms of your craft, but richly rewarding, too, in the way it expands your personal horizons and makes you ever more keenly aware of this wonderful world we all share.

Good luck to you!

RESEARCH RESOURCES AND TECHNIQUES

Reference is made throughout the text to various research resources and methods for gathering information. As a central reference point, this appendix will recapitulate most of that information as well as offer additional suggestions.

For one setting project, a single source may furnish almost all the information that's needed. For another, you may need to try several research avenues in order to come up with sufficient data to build a credible setting in your story. Here we'll consider each primary research source in its own right, touching upon the special value of each and upon specialized techniques, if any, involved in mining that source.

On-site visits almost always represent the most desirable way to get information about an area to be used as part of a story setting. Nothing quite beats being there and experiencing the place yourself. There is a freshness and immediacy to the experience that no other kind of research can quite duplicate.

The moral: If you can possibly visit an actual site, whether you plan to use the site itself or one similar to it, by all means do so.

You should try to do some homework about such a site before you visit. Studying a map, glancing through a local history, or finding something about the place in a travel guide may give you a fine running start when you get there in person. It helps amazingly to know things like which way Main Street runs or where the local college is, for example. If you know a little about the local history and problems, so much the better. The more you know ahead of time, the less time you are likely to waste getting oriented once you arrive. On most visits, time is of the essence and you simply can't afford to use half of it trying to figure out where you should go or what questions you should ask.

Don't hesitate to write ahead to possible local sources, including the chamber of commerce, the visitors' bureau if there is one, the local newspaper, and even the mayor or city manager. State when you plan to be in town, what your propject is, and the general kind of information you're seeking. Most local sources will be flattered by your interest and eager to help. It may even be possible to start your visit by interviewing one or more local experts. (See below for more on interviewing.)

When you arrive on the scene, you should be prepared with a collection of notebooks and pens or pencils, an audiotape recorder, and a videotape recorder if you have one. Plan to make notes on everything, and record as much as you can.

Finally, try to avoid the natural tendency many of us have to be shy in a new situation and to worry about bothering people, although common courtesy, of course, is always desirable. And while it is possible to make a nuisance of yourself, you will usually find local people more than happy to answer questions and give assistance. It's flattering to be told your visitor is a writer interested in using your town, area, neighborhood or business as a story setting; most people will go out of their way to be helpful in such circumstances.

Interviews are the major sources of information during onsite visits or other data-gathering expeditions. Interviewing is a minor art. I've been interviewed by people who made it a pleasurable and interesting experience, and by others whose awkwardness and lack of preparation made the interview from my standpoint both boring and irritating. You can make your interviews as much fun for your subject as they are informative for you if you will follow three basic principles: prepare ahead of time; have plans for the meeting; be professional.

Preparation for an interview is always possible to some degree, with perhaps the exception of a rare occasion when you happen to run into a source person unexpectedly and conduct an interview on the spot. But such spontaneous interviews are rare. Usually, whether you're on a field trip or meeting a local expert, you know about the interview well ahead of time.

What kind of preparations are required? They vary, but you should at least have some idea about who your source is — her name (and how to spell and pronounce it!), her job title or area of expertise, and other such fundamental biographical information. This information may be sketchy if you have written for an appointment, for example, and were unable to question anyone else about your subject's personal data. But get what you can. (As an interviewee, I have found that there are few things less likely to inspire confidence and a desire to be helpful than having an interviewer say something like, "Good morning, Mr. Brickman!" And yes, it has happened to me.)

In addition to knowing what you can about your interviewee, you should also research whatever is available about the field or area you plan to ask about. If you'll be talking to someone about local history, for example, you should have at least a smattering of information from books or brochures so that you are not totally ignorant about the subject. This not only saves time during the interview, but makes your interviewee feel more relaxed and confident in you because of your obvious preparation. (It also helps your confidence in dealing with a stranger and asking questions which may include some that might sound impertinent.)

If you are seeking other kinds of setting information — if you are planning to ask a business executive about how his company works, as a takeoff point for building a similar story setting, for example — then it helps if you go in with some idea of what the source's area of expertise is. This doesn't mean you have to understand quasar theory to interview an astronomer, but a quick trip to the library or the encyclopedia would give you some idea about quasars before you meet her, and any background is better than none.

In addition to preparation before the interview, you should also have other plans for the meeting. Obviously you should also have a list of factual setting or story-background questions written out in advance to guide you through your talk. You might also have a list of fundamental biographical facts you want to verify at some point—job title, background, telephone number where your subject might be reached, etc.

It may be that the interview will go splendidly, and quickly become a mutually enjoyable chat. That can happen when you're well prepared. But there will be other times when your interviewee is tense or impatient—or you are—and things do not go well. Having the list of prepared questions is helpful as a "fallback position" in such cases; you always have them to run through, and won't likely find yourself stuck in an uncomfortable silence while you wonder frantically what you should say.

All this, of course, is part of how you should conduct yourself before and during the interview. You should be professional.

What does that mean? In addition to preparation ahead of time and having your plans for the interview written down and in mind, it also means having a specific time and place set for the interview, being there on time, and looking presentable. Don't overdress. But don't go looking like you just crawled out of a mineshaft, either.

Once the interview begins, strive to be cool and confident. You needn't apologize for being there. Remember that it's your interview, and you can quietly control the situation.

It may be intimidating to walk into an interview with a revered local historian, for example, or with a famous doctor. The impulse may be to start apologizing for being so uninformed in the expert's field. But what you have to remember is that your subject may be an expert in her field, but you are the expert in yours. I have often told a subject something like, "I don't know a lot about quasars, but I'm a professional in my field just as you are in yours. If we work together, we can make it possible for laymen to get a much better appreciation for all this."

This is not an egotistical attitude, but simply a realistic one. You will be far superior to most of your interviewees in communication skills. They respect that, if your attitude and demeanor demonstrate that you are.

A professional attitude and conduct during an interview, in other words, means that you will not be apologetic or sycophantic. You will be cool and friendly, as relaxed as you can be, properly respectful, and organized. You will ask your questions, get your information, say thank you kindly, and use no more of the subject's valuable time than necessary.

Should you ask to tape an interview? Yes. But some sources will say no, or be so nervous about the machine that they watch it instead of you, and never get into the interview. In such situations, the recorder has to be shut off and put back in your attaché case. In any event, the recorder is no substitute for your notebook; it is at best a fall-back device used to clarify some point in your notes, or double-check the accuracy of a quote you've written down. You can't present a sound recording in your story; you have to transcribe information and recast it for story use. Notes taken at the time will show your instant reading of what's most important about the things being said. They will have none of the "hums" and "hahs" and background noise of the tape recording.

It is not necessary to know shorthand or speed writing to take good interview notes. You will be looking for information and can condense your notes. Often you will quickly jot down fragmentary facts, which are all you need for your setting.

Finally, when the interview is over—when you have the needed information or your allotted time is up—close the session promptly, express gratitude, and be on your way. It always helps to close with the suggestion that a later question might arise, and a request for permission to call or write back if such occurs.

Library sources are not as dynamic as an interview, but often are extremely vital. Some of these are mentioned in various parts of the main text, but the most common ones should be mentioned here.

Whenever you visit the library, it goes without saying that you should be armed with notebooks and a couple of ballpoint pens or pencils. Many materials can't be checked out, and you will have to make notes in the library's reading area.

Much of the following will be old hat to you if you are a regular user of your local public library, but if you haven't visited the library very often, or are possibly intimidated by it, then it's probably time to get reacquainted.

Libraries of medium size or larger have long since been computerized. For a person unfamiliar with such systems, walking into the lobby and being confronted by video display terminals rather than the old, familiar card catalogs, can be off-putting. But cards and computers work similarly, usually being cross-indexed by subject matter, titles and authors' names. A few minutes' work with either system will set you at ease. And librarians usually are most eager to be of assistance.

Travel guides, atlases and local or regional histories can be found in even smaller libraries. These are always worth checking into. You may find specialized materials such as genealogical collections which sometimes contain rare old photographs. (Some libraries have collections of old photos that can give you priceless insights into an area's history.) Encyclopedias may provide good general information and old newspaper files may be most helpful. Larger libraries will contain extensive microfilm collections of many older archives and collections. The Draper collection, for example, is a massive collection of documents and written interviews pertaining to the early history of Ohio, Michigan, Wisconsin and Indiana; filling hundreds of rolls of microfilm, its home is at the University of Wisconsin in Madison, Wisconsin. But copies are available in numerous other libraries. Your librarian may be the easiest source for information about such materials.

Don't overlook the periodicals room in your library; it may contain local or regional magazines with just the information you want. There will also probably be a subject cross-index to more recent magazines if it's a larger library, and this might quickly send you to a magazine article that you did not know about.

When checking any library source, of course, carefully study the footnotes and bibliographies; these can often lead you to the titles of other source materials. And if some of these are not available locally, ask about getting them through an interlibrary loan.

If you check a book or periodical out of the library, remember that it is still incumbent upon you to make notes on information you may wish to use in constructing your story setting. Taking a book to the local copy shop and duplicating many pages is in violation of federal copyright law, and even if you find an unscrupulous copy shop that will do it for you, you should resist the temptation. Writers, of all people, should be keenly aware that unauthorized copying of printed material is not only illegal, but grossly unethical. Information from a publication can be used, but such use without giving credit to the source is unethical. Copying someone's exact literary style violates copyright.

If you are planning a major piece of fiction in a certain setting which requires that considerable research material be used over a considerable period of time, you may not want to be restricted by the library's limited borrowing time. Or you may learn that there is an edition of a book published later than the copy in the library's possession. In such cases you may turn to other sources of information.

Commercial sources is just a fancy phrase meaning your local bookstores. These stores will have sections devoted to broad categories such as history, travel, sociology, etc. By visiting a few of them you will quickly learn which one has the best specialized sections.

You may find books at the store which are not in your library. I will be surprised if you don't, as all libraries seem to be strapped for funds and behind in their acquisitions. If you buy books, be sure to keep your receipt for possible tax-deduction purposes. If you're like me, you'll buy only books that you can see will have long-term research value to you, but that won't keep you from buying quite a few as you begin to build your research library.

Many colleges and universities have presses which specialize in certain areas of information. The University of Oklahoma Press, for example, has for years published many fine histories and biographies involving the western frontier, and not just Oklahoma-related items. Some of the best books currently in print about gold mining and outlawry in Montana have been published by Oklahoma. In like manner, the University of Nebraska Press has published many very fine books about Native

American history and lore. Most bookstores will either stock some of these specialized university press titles, or have access to their (as well as commercial publishers') catalogs. They'll also have a list of books currently in print, probably on microfiche, and can check specific titles and publishers for you.

Just browsing a good bookstore will sometimes reveal a magazine or a book you didn't know existed. Don't forget to browse the travel section, especially. Such books as the Fodors travel guides or the Michelin guides include detailed maps, brief histories and descriptions, and wonderful photos that can give a feel for a place.

Another commercial source, often overlooked, is your local travel agency. They're in the business of making reservations and selling tickets, so I wouldn't expect one of their busy (commission) agents to spend much time answering your questions, but most agencies have racks of tourist-luring brochures and maps free for the asking. Invariably such materials include an address where you can write for additional information.

Government sources of information for story settings range from your local county or state agricultural agent to national and even international organizations. Your city hall or courthouse might be the place to start. Is there some kind of agricultural extension service available? You may not want to know much about farming, but maybe your story setting includes a backyard flower garden; extension service offices often have tremendous amounts of information available in pamphlet form for such activities as this, too. Almost surely there is a local Civil Defense office of some kind. There are dozens and dozens of CD brochures available on everything from drinking water to weather forecasting to nuclear radiation. There may be an extensive library of area legal documents somewhere, and these could provide setting information in the form of history that you could get no other way.

In larger cities you can call a United States Government number to order government pamphlets of all kinds. Some are free, none are expensive. There is even a document you can buy which lists all the other documents available. This is a valuable resource because a myriad of federal agencies are in the publishing business.

The United Nations is a gold mine of printed information on matters of industry, health and science around the world. The organization's materials can be mail-ordered out of New York. If you are looking for factual data to be used as part of the setting in a story set abroad, the UN may be your best source, and again the cost is reasonable.

Most government agencies of the kind we're talking about here have public information as a priority part of their agenda. (If you were head of a federal government agency dependent on taxpayer support for existence, you would want to tell the taxpayers all about your operations and expertise, wouldn't you?) A simple letter to an organization such as NASA (National Aeronautics and Space Administration) or NOAA (National Oceanic and Atmospheric Adminstration, including what we once called the weather bureau) is likely to inundate you with information if you ask for it. The Department of Agriculture is another gold mine.

Computer research is another possible avenue of setting information. A number of standard library-type sources such as encyclopedias are online with major computer database services such as CompuServe or Prodigy. If you are heavily into electronic communications via the computer, there are specialized databases of all kinds. You may also be interested in commercially available computer programs available on floppy disk (or on CD-ROM); these let you "dial up" deeply detailed information on various regions of the world, or even major cities. More of such material is coming onto the market all the time.

Correspondence may go well beyond sending for brochures and pamphlets. If you locate the name of a company or individual that might have information useful for your setting work, it never hurts to write a letter asking specific questions or seeking an interview. I had a cordial response to such a routine letter of inquiry and enjoyed months of letters back and forth as I explored a topic in far greater detail than I ever imagined possible.

In a letter of this type, it's important to say who you are

and how you're qualified (as a writer, not in their field!), generally and briefly what your project is, and to provide a sample specific question or two. Then sit back and see what returns. Sometimes it's a joyous surprise. (Once I got a thirty-pound box of materials from a scientist at NOAA, for example.)

Local experts are another source of setting information not to be overlooked. It may be the old codger sitting on the park bench downtown who knows the town's history better than anyone. Or it might be a woman living nearby who has devoted half her life to learning all she can about a city and a lifestyle halfway around the planet. By all means ask your friends and associates if they know of anyone in the area you're researching. Ask at the library as well, as librarians often know such experts. Such a person will sometimes give you not only good factual information, but a sense of the feeling of a place or time, anecdotes, a loving look at something or someplace otherwise unavailable.

In all cases, whatever kind of research you do, keep good notes. Develop a standardized method of hanging onto them, be it file cards, file folders, computer disk, or whatever. Learn to honor research, and it will be your best companion now and for all your writing career.

NANCY BERLAND'S SETTING RESEARCH FORM

Nancy Berland is an Oklahoma novelist who is active in the Romance Writers of America. This form is one she uses in workshops she gives around the country.

Copyright © 1992, Nancy Berland. Used by permission of Nancy Berland.

Date/time/season of visit _____ mid Jan — Spring _____

City/town name _____ Auburn _____ State _____ NY _____

County/Township/Borough (indicate which) _____

County seat? yes _____ X _____ no _____

Area of state (northeast, northwest, panhandle, etc.) _____ NE _____

Community's population _____

County population _____ 80,000 100,000 _____

Form of government _____

Location of city hall or seat of local government _____ only ¼ mile from County _____

Impressions

Three adjectives which most closely describe your first impression of community (friendly, fast-paced life, sleepy community, etc.) _____
_____ old boys network _____

General attitude of citizens (friendly, snobbish, etc.) _____

_____

_____

How would you describe town's populace? (Old-timers who sit on street corners? Yuppies? Blue collar? Well-educated? Minorities? Mention all groups noticed.) ___ Most rooted here ___

_____ not mobility _____

_____

Sensory Impressions

Odors you detected in the air (specify day/time smelled) _____

_____ Summer - sludge 1998! Following wed ___

of the city hall mtg I go to mtg.

Sky and air quality (Overcast—is this typical during this season? Smoggy, foggy, clouds—what kind? Clear?) _____

_____

_____

If weather affected your skin, note how _____

_____

_____

Weather on day you visited (temperature, direction of wind and velocity—general) _____

_____

_____

This area's unique climate conditions (electrical storms, hurricanes, ice storms, etc.) ___ finger lake ___

a lot water ways

safe towns

Foods unique to the area and your reaction to these _____

_____

_____

Sounds you noticed (testing of jet engines, freight train rumblings, sonic booms, plant whistles, etc.) _____

_____

_____

Other sensory information unique to the area _____

_____

_____

Physical Features

Predominant geographical features (mountains, buttes, mesas, lakes, rivers, canyons, etc., noting specific names if these have been utilized as recreational areas) ___ *F.L., Oswego* _____

_____

_____

Layout of community (town square, streets intersecting at right angles mainly, streets radiating like spokes from central point, as in Washington, D.C.) ___ *wide road at N/S street* ___
___ *up town Downtown* ___
___ *battle for attracting business* ___

Street surfaces (note differences and where) _____
___ *try to improve/decorate in street.* ___
___ *- SVan mostly run by women* ___

Predominant architectural forms (Victorian, A-frames, adobe huts, high-rise apartments. Note types for different socioeconomic groups)
___ *City Hall - pillar/nice* ___
___ *Canby - plain 1960's bldg (old office area)* ___

Predominant landmarks/statues, noting materials of man-made structures _____
___ *WWII stone installed (after or before)* ___
___ *me losing 1996 front of C.G.* ___

SETTING

Shopping centers _____

_____

_____

Local amusements (parks, tourist attractions, noting locations) _____

_____ Oswosco , Seward , Harriet Tubman

_____ cintright

Nearby communities _Skaneatles_____

___most villages/_____

_____

Public transportation & name/locations of terminals/airports, etc. _____

Centro bus _____ NO _____

_____

Flora, Fauna and Such Stuff

Soil type/texture/color _____ green _____

_____

Types of trees (note if in bloom) _____ leaves _____

_____

_____

Flowers (same info, note colors) _____

_____

_____

Observations about animals _____

Common local birds/fish/insects _____

_____

_____

Speech Patterns & Miscellaneous

Note unusual speech patterns, including age and socioeconomic group

of those speaking _____ are ASL _____

_____

_____

clarify job descript.
parents to town
friends

Gathering places for local citizens, including old-timers and young people old timers' coffee at McDonald evening

Hunter, fire dept

Syracuse – lawyers / DR / Politicians

Local residents are proud of what aspects of this community?

Spiritual / values

strong connections, know family of family

Names of local newspapers/magazines, including contact persons for each Citizen – Sue a...

Post Standard – Dave

Local booksellers

Local book distributor

DUCK Race by Club K+C or Lions

Community festivals/fairs/holiday celebrations Tomatoe festival

C.C. fairground, Parades at Downtown

after Thanksgiving / memorial

Names of friends you made during your visit (with phone numbers/ addresses) you may wish to consult later Margaret, only

grewup together

Kind of energy utility (natural gas, electricity, etc.)

Note: Nancy Berland grants permission to reproduce this form for personal use but not for publication. For questions, call Nancy at 405-721-2571.

INDEX

A

Accuracy, importance of, 17-22
Action
  immediate, setting changes that
    demand, 66, 69
  swift, description during, 115-123
Adjectives and adverbs, avoiding
  description based on, 134-135
Artistic license, 29-35

B

Background, of story, 125-128
Big Sky Revenge, 95-96, 98-100
Bookstore, research at, 130, 161-162

C

Character
  cast against setting, 77-78
  change in, using setting to achieve,
    78-83
  influence of setting on, 5-6, 73-75
  setting as, 84
  viewpoint, facts observed by, 24-26
  See also Hero
Character expectations, overturning, 66,
  68-69
Clinton, Jeff, 95-96, 98-100
Contrast, adding, for emphasis, 138-139

D

Darker Than Amber, 2-3
Description
  using purple prose in, 136-137
  vivid, 8-9, 12
  See also Detail, Style
Detail
  expansion of, for unity, 53-54
  of new setting, when to avoid, 57-59
  repetition of, 12-13, 107-108

  too much, avoiding, 22-24, 97-100
Dialogue
  influence of setting on, 2
  inventing, for real people, 33
  See also Jargon, period
Double Fault, 111-114, 116-123
du Maurier, Daphne, 2-3

E

Editing, learning by, 148
Ending, mood and symbolism in, 108-109
Errors. *See* Accuracy, importance of
Exercise
  observation, 146-147
  in regional setting, 132
  self-examination, 92-93
  using factual data in setting, 141-146
  using setting for unity, 60-61
  using setting to change character, 83-84

F

Facts, observation of, by viewpoint
  character, 24-26
Factual data, in setting, exercise in,
  141-146
Files
  for background facts, 36-37
  for ongoing study of setting, 150-153

G

Genre
  historical, 44-45
  romance, 40-42, 72
  science fiction, 45-47
  suspense, 42-44
  western 28, 38-40, 71-72

H

Hearing impressions, 10

Hero
 romance, 72
 western, 71-72
Historical society, research at, 129-130
Historicals, conventions in, 44-45

I

Interviews, conducting, for research, 130-
 131, 156-159

J

Jargon, period, 34
Journal, keeping, for ongoing study of
 setting, 150-153

L

Libel, 30-32
Library, research at, 26-27, 129, 159-161
Location, changing, of real events, 33-34

M

MacDonald, John D., 2-3
Markets, studying, 47
Middle, maintaining mood and unity in,
 107-108
Miles, John, 32-33, 66-69
Mood
 darkening, to enhance tension, 66-68
 and viewpoint, 101-104
Mystery, creating, to enhance tension,
 66-68

N

Night Hunters, The, 32-33, 66-69
Novel, unity in, 48-50

O

Objective correlative, defined, 102
Observation
 exercise in, 146-147
 learning, to hone description skills,
 139-140
Opening, establishing mood in, 104-107

P

Passive voice, avoiding, 135
People, real, in fiction, 30-33
Plot

advancement of, 62-66
 impact of setting on, 5, 56-57
Point of view. *See* Viewpoint
Protagonist. *See* Character, Hero
Prototypes, and stereotypes, 75-77

R

Reader, emotions of, and story mood,
 102-103
Reader, expectations of
 fulfilling, 38, 40, 42, 44-45
 at story opening, 107
Reader involvement, enhancement of, 4
Rebecca, 2-3
References, ongoing, to aspects of setting,
 54-55
Regensburg Legacy, The, 43
Repetition
 power of, 69-70
 of setting description, 52-53
 of single element in setting, 50-52
Research, 26-27, 128-131
 at bookstores, 130, 161-162
 computer, 130, 163
 by correspondence, 130, 163-164
 government sources for, 130, 162-163
 interviews, 130-131, 156-159
 library, 26-27, 129, 159-161
 through personal contact, 76-77, 126-
 129, 155
 See also Setting, history of
Romance
 conventions in, 40-42
 hero of, 72

S

Science fiction, conventions in, 45-47
Sensory descriptions, 9-11
Setting
 casting against, 77-78
 changes inside, 64-66
 as character, 84
 contributions of, 3-6
 emphasizing, in new way, 62-64
 history of, 126-128
 isolated, 38-39
 new, when to avoid details of, 57-59
 new aspect of, 64

regional, 125-126
and theme, 85-89
using, to change character, 78-83
See also Description, Detail
Setting Research Form, 152, 165-169
exercise using, 141-146
Sight impressions, 9-10
Smell, sense of, 10-11
Stereotypes, and prototypes, 75-77
Story
ending of, 108-109
middle of, 107-108
opening of, 104-107
Story ideas, 89-92
Story meaning, 85-89
Style
influence of setting on, 2-3
simple, 133-135
Suspense
conventions in, 42-44
influence of setting on, 5
Symbol, using, for unity, 50-59, 107-108

T

Tactile sensations, 11
Techniques, unifying, 50-57, 107-108
Tension, enhancement of, 66-69
Theme, and setting, 6, 85-89

Timing, changing, of real events, 33-34
Tip sheets, defined, 72
Touch, sense of. *See* Tactile sensations
Town, inventing, 29-30
Twister, 16-17

U

Unity
influence of setting on, 4-5
in long stories, 48-50

V

Verb, compound vs. simple past tense,
135-136
Viewpoint, 100
character, vs. omniscient, 14-17
and mood, 101-104
omniscient, 94-96, 105-106
restricted, 97
staying in, while moving, 110-115
switching, to provide details, 98-100
Voice, passive, 135

W

Western
conventions in, 28, 38-40
hero of, 71-72
Winemakers, The, 6
Writer, admired, learning from, 147